THE GREAT BETRAYAL

THE
GREAT
BETRAYAL

ERNLE BRADFORD

DORSET PRESS
New York

This edition published by Dorset Press,
a division of Marboro Books Corporation,
by arrangement with
Brandt and Brandt.
1990 Dorset Press

ISBN 0-88029-598-8

Printed in the United States of America
M 9 8 7 6 5 4 3 2 1

To the memory of
JOHN DAVENPORT
Aut Ararim Parthus bibet aut Germania Tigrim,
quam nostro illius labatur pectore voltus.

PREFACE

In one of the most despicable acts in history, the Venetians and the Crusaders sacked and destroyed the Bastion of the West. The division and isolation of eastern from western Europe derives from their act. The consequences of the fall of Constantinople in 1204 to the army of the Fourth Crusade are felt to this day. The dismemberment of the eastern Empire by the Venetians and the Crusaders not only let the Turks into Europe; it led subsequently to the 'Balkan problem'; and ultimately produced a favourable climate for the current division of eastern and western Europe. All stems from this one tragic event—the diversion of the Fourth Crusade to Constantinople.

For nine hundred years, this great Christian city commanding the trade routes between Asia, Russia and Europe was the bastion and guardian of civilisation. Behind the sheltering arm of the Byzantine Empire, the petty states of Europe were able to drag themselves out of the confusion and chaos left behind by the wreck of the western Roman Empire.

As George Orwell wrote in another context: "... men can only be highly civilised while other men, inevitably less civilised, are there to guard and feed them." The civilisation of Constantinople itself was only made possible by its soldiers, who continued "watchful on the rampart", guarding the frontiers of the Empire against the constant irruptions from the hostile East and the barbarous North. Similarly, the growth of western Europe was only made possible by the fact that, between it and the pressing hordes of Asia and Russia, lay the strong arm of Byzantium, the God-guarded City, with its armies, its complicated system of treaties and its brilliant use of diplomatic subtlety and evasion.

Two questions must be asked: why did the West attack Constantinople; and why have western historians subsequently tended to play down the whole issue? The answer to the first question is threefold. The Crusaders had a long-standing grudge against the Byzantine Empire because it tended to regard the Levant as its lost province (which indeed it was), and tried therefore to use the Crusaders as mercenaries to effect its own interests. Secondly, and far more important, there was the commercial grudge of Venice, which had enjoyed large trading privileges in the East—only to desire more. Thirdly, the Normans had been at loggerheads with Constantinople ever since their conquest of parts of formerly Byzantine Southern Italy and Sicily in the eleventh century. But it was the commercial grudge of Venice, aided and abetted by the Machiavellian brilliance of Doge Dandolo, that finally brought about the ruin of the city and the Empire. The Fourth Crusade was predominantly a French enterprise, but it was Venetian cunning that diverted the Crusade to the place where it could best serve Venetian interests.

The reason why western historians have tended to ignore, or cursorily treated, this disastrous series of events is that it has proved an embarrassment to them—particularly if they were of the Roman Catholic persuasion. The destruction of a great Christian civilisation (and of an empire which had so long held both Pagans and Moslems at bay) by 'Soldiers of Christ' destined for the Holy Land, is not an edifying subject. Although the Pope can be excused from any complicity in the plot, yet it was the knowledge that Innocent III would like to see the Orthodox Church brought into union with Rome which gave the plotters sufficient confidence to invade Byzantine territory.

Some historians, also, have taken their cue from Edward Gibbon, whose dislike of Byzantium and its civilisation is notorious. Yet even Gibbon is forced to lament the results of the Fourth Crusade, calculating the loot taken from the city as being worth "seven times the annual revenue of England". As for the destruction of works of art and literature, Gibbon remarks that "the pilgrims were not solicitous to save or transport the volumes of an unknown tongue . . . The literature of the Greeks had almost centred in the metropolis; and, without

compiling the extent of our loss, we may drop a tear over the
libraries that have perished in the triple fire of Constantinople."

We may drop more than a tear for the loss of bronzes,
marbles, great statuary groups, priceless mosaics, paintings,
icons and jewelled reliquaries that were destroyed by the
barbarous Crusaders. The burning of the great library of
Alexandria by the Arabs in A.D. 640 has occasioned many an
historical lament. What may one not feel over the destruction
of Constantinople's treasures in 1204?

The contemporary Greek historian Nicetas said of the Crusaders, "They have spared neither the living nor the dead.
They have insulted God; they have outraged his servants;
they have exhausted every variety of sin." The behaviour of
the Christian conquerors in 1204 contrasts unfavourably even
with that of the Turks, when they took the city in 1453. More
hatred seems to have been displayed by these Christian
conquerors towards their co-religionists than was to be shown by
the Moslems some two hundred years later to their religious
enemies. It is a depressing fact that Moslems were usually more
tolerant than Christians in their dealings with captured cities
and conquered territories. In the history of religions, more
intolerance has been displayed by Christians than by the
followers of any other Faith.

If Pope Innocent III can be acquitted of any share in the
crime of the Crusaders against Constantinople and the Orthodox Church, he was soon to show that this was not due to any
element of tolerance or loving-kindness in his nature. Only
four years later, in March 1208, he was to initiate a Crusade
against the French Catharist heretics, which resulted in the
massacre of tens of thousands of men, women and children. As
his legate, Arnold the Abbot of Cîteaux, was then to say: "Kill
them all! God will know his own!"

The literature concerning the fall of Constantinople to the
Turks in 1453 is extensive, but this is not the case regarding the
city's conquest by the Crusaders. Among English historians,
only Sir Edwin Pears in 1886 has fully analysed the causes and
the consequences of the Fourth Crusade. Since that time
further material has come to light, while the shifting pattern of

world history has shown even more clearly how disastrous was the result of this Crusade. To the nineteenth-century historian its worst product was to have let the Turks into Europe. But, many years after the collapse of the Ottoman Empire, it is possible to see that the subsequent 'Balkanisation' of eastern Europe stems not so much from the Turkish as from the Latin conquest, which alone made the other possible.

It is not difficult to see why Turkish historians have laid so great an emphasis on the capture of Constantinople in 1453. The aggrandisement of the Sultan Mehmet II was naturally to be desired by his contemporaries, and it has continued to the present day. But the fact remains that when the Turks captured the city, it was moribund. Practically nothing remained of what had once been the great Byzantine Empire. The Turks were already on the banks of the Danube, and the fall of Constantinople had been inevitable for many years. Even the victorious Sultan commented on the city's derelict appearance. Vast acres of it were in ruins long before the Turkish army swept in through the breached walls. Vegetable gardens, trees and sown fields grew over the sites of forgotten palaces, roads had reverted to dust tracks, and churches were deserted or roofless.

The conquest of Constantinople by Mehmet II in 1453 was something of a hollow affair. It is true that the city provided a convenient capital for 'Turkey in Europe', and that its fall was important in terms of morale (for the sacred city of the Christians was something that had long been regarded as an ultimate reward for the Faithful). But Constantinople and the Byzantine Empire had received their death-blow from the Fourth Crusade two and a half centuries before.

It cannot be denied that, at the time the Fourth Crusade was diverted to Constantinople, the Byzantine Empire was corrupted by a succession of indifferent rulers, and weakened by the onslaught of the Seljuk Turks in Asia Minor. Nevertheless the Empire had been through weak phases before, had survived and had re-emerged to carry on its great tradition. For the Byzantine achievement is something that can only be comprehended when the price at which it was bought is also fully understood. As N. H. Baynes wrote in his introduction to *Byzantium*: "It is hardly an exaggeration to say that the civilisation of western Europe is a by-product of the Byzantine Empire's will to survive."

Nineteenth-century historians found the date of the Turkish conquest of Constantinople a convenient one for marking the close of the Middle Ages. It was suggested that after 1453 an influx of Byzantine learning, arts and crafts into western Europe contrived to fertilise the Renaissance. More is now known about the origins of the Renaissance, and it is quite apparent that a slow and steady emigration of talent from the East to the West had begun several centuries before this date—had begun, indeed, almost immediately after the Latin conquest of the city in 1204. As Sir Steven Runciman has remarked in *The Fall of Constantinople, 1453*: "There is no point at which we can say that the medieval world changed itself into the modern world. Long before 1453 the movement that is called the Renaissance was under way in Italy and the Mediterranean world . . ."

It was in the centuries immediately following upon the Latin conquest that men of learning and ability began to leave the decaying city, and turn towards the rising mercantile stars of Venice, Genoa, Pisa and Amalfi. No great art-treasures from the long centuries of Byzantium reached Europe after the Turkish conquest. Such as remained—and they were few enough—stayed in the city to inspire the Turkish conquerors, while the influence of great buildings like Santa Sophia continued to permeate the Near East for centuries to come.

All the great art-treasures of Constantinople (excepting the vast number which had been destroyed, or melted down for coin) reached Europe after the return of the Venetians and the Crusaders in the years immediately after 1204. The famous Quadriga of St. Mark's is no more than loot from Constantinople. The Treasury of St. Mark's itself is a monument to Venetian piracy—and even the famous Pala d'Oro (within which rests the body of St. Mark) is decorated with loot stemming from the Fourth Crusade. There is hardly a major cathedral in western Europe which does not boast some reliquary or enamelled trophy dating from the sack of Constantinople by the Crusaders.

The ironic result of the Fourth Crusade was that the Crusaders—who had set out to conquer Egypt, with the view to freeing the Holy Land—facilitated the conquest of eastern Europe by Islam. Duped by the Venetians, betrayed by their own leaders, and enslaved by their passions, they destroyed an irreplaceable legacy: the unity that Byzantine civilisation had constructed out of many races, territories and scattered islands. The greatest irony of all was that these 'Christian Soldiers' ensured that the schism between Rome and the Orthodox Church would endure for centuries. Technical 'reconciliations' have taken place in subsequent years, but most members of the eastern Churches continue to regard Rome as the great apostate and eternal enemy.

Political, human and religious motives diverted the Fourth Crusade. As George Meredith wrote:

No villain need be! Passions spin the plot:
We are betrayed by what is false within.

There were indeed 'villains' involved in this tragic episode of human history, but they were petty compared to what they achieved. Christians from France, Belgium, Germany and Italy, "betrayed by what is false within", destroyed for centuries any potential unity of Christendom and Europe.

This is a calamitous story, but it contains a moral for our own time: western civilisation and culture are more likely to collapse from internal dissension than from external pressure. The enemy is within. It is a hydra with many heads, but three predominate—Stupidity, Envy and Greed. The destruction of Constantinople and its Empire is an appalling example of what can result from political opportunism and narrow patriotism. It is not necessary to look very far in the western world at this moment to see similar dangers arising from similar misguided policies.

I have deliberately ended this book with the fall of the city, dealing only very briefly with the subsequent Latin Empire.

The restoration of the Byzantine Emperors and the second fall of the city to the Ottoman Turks are subjects which have engaged many scholars and authorities. I am deeply indebted to Sir Edwin Pears' work, *The Fall of Constantinople* (*The Story of the Fourth Crusade*), published in 1886—the only full work on this subject in the English language. I agree with most of his concl·sions, although he was perhaps too inclined to see Pope Innocent III as entirely blameless. It must not be forgotten that the Pope's first reaction on hearing of the city's capture was to write an enthusiastic letter to the Emperor Baldwin, commending him and the Crusaders for what they had done. It was only when the Pope heard in detail of how Constantinople had been taken, and how its people, priests and churches had been treated, that he wrote his famous denunciation of the Crusaders and Venetians. In a brief appendix I refer to the sources used in this book, with my estimation of their reliability. The asterisks in the text refer to the Notes.

A short bibliography indicates some other books and sources which students may find useful. As always, I am deeply indebted to the London Library which, by allowing me to study in my own home, has made research possible for someone who does not have the resources of a university library at his disposal. My thanks go to Miss Jocelyn Porter for her assistance over contemporary pictures and illustrations and, as always, to my wife for her work on maps and charts, and for her endurance over manuscripts and proofs. Finally, I would like to thank Mr. S. N. Yamut for his kindness and hospitality during my stays in Istanbul and Bursa, and for the long hours he spent driving me through Asian and European Turkey, Bulgaria and Jugoslavia.

E. B.

CONTENTS

And every shipmaster, and all the company in ships, and sailors, and as many as trade by sea, stood afar off,

And cried when they saw the smoke of her burning, saying, What city is like unto this great city!

And they cast dust on their heads, and cried, weeping and wailing, saying, Alas, Alas, that great city, wherein were made rich all that had ships in the sea by reason of her costliness! For in one hour is she made desolate.

Revelation: XVIII, 17–19

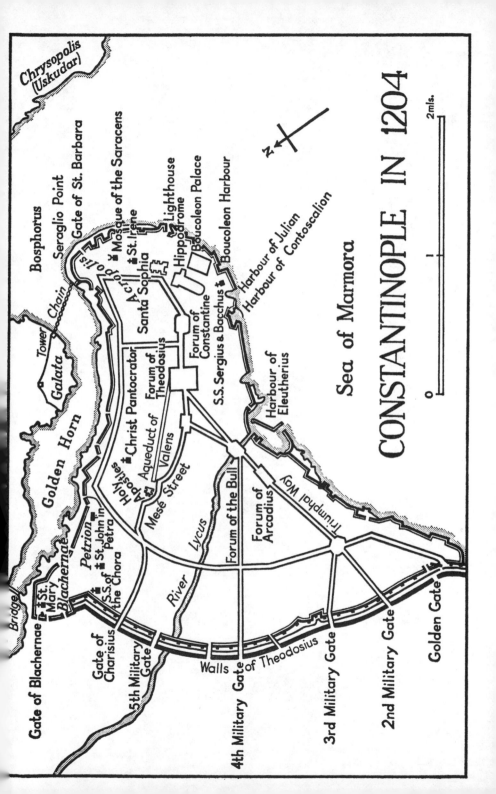

CONSTANTINOPLE IN 1204

Chrysopolis (Uskudar)

Bosphorus

Seraglio Point

Gate of St. Barbara

Mosque of the Saracens

St. Irene

Acropolis

Santa Sophia

Lighthouse

Hippodrome

Boucoleon Palace

Boucoleon Harbour

Harbour of Julian

Harbour of Contoscalion

Sea of Marmora

Tower Chain

Galata

Golden Horn

Bridge

St. Mary Blachernae

Gate of Blachernae

Petrion

S.S. of St. John in the Chora

Holy Apostles

Christ Pantocrator

Aqueduct of Valens

Forum of Theodosius

Forum of Constantine

Mese Street

S.S. Sergius & Bacchus

Harbour of Eleutherius

River Lycus

Forum of the Bull

Forum of Arcadius

Triumphal Way

Gate of Charisius

5th Military Gate

4th Military Gate

Walls of Theodosius

3rd Military Gate

2nd Military Gate

Golden Gate

N

2 mls.

0   1

I

THE CRUSADERS SIGHT THE CITY

It was the morning of June 22nd, 1203. The sea was calm, the wind southerly, and the coastline of Asia shimmered under the June sun. A great fleet under way is one of the most moving sights in the world, and the fleet which was now gliding northwards under oar and sail through the mile-wide confines of the Dardanelles was larger than any that even these embattled waters had ever known. It consisted of over 450 warships, merchantmen and transports—not counting the innumerable small vessels that followed in its wake. "To the east the Straits seemed to blossom with the decorated warships, galleys and merchantmen. It was something so beautiful as to remember all one's life . . ." So wrote the Comte de Villehardouin when, as an old man, he recorded the greatest experience of his youth—the advance of the fleet that bore the Fourth Crusade towards the city of Constantinople, the capital of the Byzantine Empire.

The piping of a galley overseer's whistle, as he issued his orders to the rowers, etched itself on the still air as sharply as a burin on fine silver. Every now and then, the dull boom of a gong revealed where one of the galleys was raising or lowering the stroke in order to maintain formation. Sails "seen like blown white flowers at sea" were broadcast over the blue acres of the Marmora and, like flowers, they opened and closed as the prevailing speed of the convoy dictated.

Fifty galleys formed the backbone of this armada. The officers' quarters in their sterns were decorated with elaborate scroll-work and gilded carvings, while their bows swaggered with carved and painted figures above the lean underwater rams that had changed little since the fleets of classical Greece.

Above the dark line of oar-ports (where the rowers toiled in their sweat and stench) the rubbing-strakes of the galleys were bright with gold. The bulwarks of plain wood that rose three or four feet above the level of the upper decks were in startling contrast to the rest of the vessels' decoration. Spaced at irregular intervals along them hung the shields of the knights embarked aboard, the blazons and quarterings of the great families of northern Europe.

Behind the lean greyhound galleys—the finest warships of their period—came hundreds of transports and merchant ships, their square sails filling and emptying as they wallowed forward with the southerly swell under their blunt sterns. Most awkward of all were the *huissiers* or *palanders*. Bluff-bowed and rounded aft, in the fashion of Adriatic vessels, these were transport landing-craft specially designed to carry men and horses. Although they were now closed for sea-going, one could make out the square disembarkation ports cut in their sides (marked by their fringes of oakum and tar) whence the war-horses would be led down ramps on to the invaded shore.

Larger than the *palanders* but hardly less gainly were the broad-beamed merchantmen which formed the bulk of the fleet. Laden with stores, victuals and war-armament—siege-engines, mangonels, ballistas and spear-hurling catapults—they trailed astern dependent solely on the wind. Behind them again, and scattered all round the horizon as far as the eye could see, there dipped and flashed the lateen sails of small boats. These belonged to the independent adventurers, Italian and Jewish merchants, and pirates from the Aegean Islands. They hovered astern of the Fourth Crusade like seagulls that follow a fishing-fleet for their pickings of gut and offal.

Behind it the fleet left a wake of fear—the island of Andros over-run, the coastline at the mouth of the Dardanelles pillaged and the ancient city of Abydos on the verge of starvation, for the Crusading army had stripped the countryside of the harvest. Abydos, famed for the loves of Hero and Leander, had surrendered within a few hours of the advance guard coming ashore—"Like men," the Comte de Villehardouin harshly remarked, "who have not sufficient courage to defend themselves."

It might be wondered what possible chance of defence the citizens of this small port could have had against so overpowering an army and so large a fleet. The surprising thing is that they should ever have been expected to defend their city against an army that "had taken up the Cross" to prosecute the war against the enemies of the Christian Faith. The inhabitants of Abydos were neither Turks nor Moslems, but Greeks of the Orthodox Christian Faith. Their city was one of the toll-gates of the Byzantine Empire. They were citizens of a nation that had fought against the Turks, and against all the barbarian invaders of eastern Europe ever since the Emperor Constantine had founded his capital on the Bosphorus nearly nine centuries before.

Villehardouin commented that everything which the Crusaders took from the neighbourhood of the Dardanelles and from Abydos was paid for, "so that the people of the city did not lose even the smallest coin in exchange". He was far from consistent, however, for he had earlier suggested that he had always known the object of the Crusade was not the one which the Pope had blessed. Describing the fleet after it had left Corfu on its way to the Aegean Sea, he wrote: "It was a more wonderful sight than has ever been seen before. As far as the eye could reach, the sea was covered with the sails of ships and galleys. Our hearts were filled with joy, *and we felt sure that our armament could undertake the conquest of the world*." These were hardly the words of a man who would be concerned whether the citizens of a small port were compensated for everything that was taken from them.

The history of the Fourth Crusade has been described as "a history of the predominance of the lay motive, of the attempt of the papacy to escape from that predominance, and to establish its old direction of the crusade, and of the complete failure of its attempt".* Certainly Pope Innocent III, who had promoted the Crusade, had intended that its goal should be Egypt, since Egypt was now the centre of Mahommedan power. It was also (something that could not fail to be of interest to an

Italian, son of the noble Trasimondo family) the country most important to Italy's mercantile communities on account of its proximity to the Red Sea and to the commerce of the Indian Ocean. If the Pope blessed the Crusade, it was always with the understanding that its direction should be towards Egypt. Even now, as the great fleet moved slowly through the Sea of Marmora towards the Bosphorus, messengers were carrying the news to Rome that there could be no doubt the Crusade had left Corfu with the intention of proceeding to Constantinople. The knights and nobles and men-at-arms had turned aside from their holy war against the infidel. By now they should long ago have disembarked and been engaged on the hot sands, and or in the steamy delta-land of Egypt, against the enemies of the Faith.

Like the famous First Crusade of 1097, the Fourth was predominantly a French enterprise. Tibald, Count of Champagne, had been chosen as its leader, but when he had died in May 1201, Boniface, Marquis of Montferrat, was elected his successor. Hugo, Count of St. Paul, Baldwin, Count of Flanders, and Geoffrey de Villehardouin, Marshal of Champagne, were prominent among the leaders. While the bulk of the lesser nobility and men-at-arms were French or French feudatories, the fleet that carried them and the galleys that escorted them were Venetian. Boniface might be the nominal head of the expedition, but to all intents and purposes the man whose galley led the fleet, and whose ability and intelligence controlled it, was Enrico Dandolo, Doge of Venice.

Over eighty years old, almost totally blind, Enrico Dandolo had been elected Doge in 1193. He had already proved himself one of the most capable and energetic rulers that his city had known. One of his greatest successes had been in restoring the Venetian authority over the Dalmatians (who had rebelled against Venice under the protection of the King of Hungary). In this campaign he had failed to capture the important seaport of Zara—but this was an omission which he rectified only a few months before, when, in November 1202, Zara had fallen to the combined forces of the Crusaders and the Venetians. The city had been razed to the ground, and its walls, towers and palaces destroyed. With this ruthless achievement behind him, the Doge now viewed the prospect of a campaign which, if successful, would secure for his city the inheritance of an empire, and would render his name immortal in the annals of Venice.

His aim was no less than to place upon the throne of the ancient Byzantine Empire a pretender who would be permanently in debt to his protectors, or (and this the Doge may secretly have hoped) if this proved impossible, to capture Constantinople itself and take for the Venetian Republic in his grandiloquent phrase "one half and one quarter of the Roman Empire". The hero of one country is almost inevitably the villain of another. If Enrico Dandolo has deserved well of Venice, the story of the Fourth Crusade may lead to the thought that he has deserved less well of Europe and the world.

The pretext for the diversion of the crusaders from their legitimate destination was aboard the Doge's galley. As the ships fanned out into the Sea of Marmora, Alexius, the pretender to the throne of Byzantium, was nearing his goal. He waited to be proclaimed Emperor in his capital, Constantinople, with the backing of the same Crusading swords that had given Zara to the Doge. Insignificant though he was as a human being, the ambitions of this young man were to lead to a tragedy beyond all measure.

Alexius's claim to the throne was based on the fact that his father, Isaac II, had been the Emperor for ten years until deposed by his brother in 1195. Isaac, who has been described as "one of the weakest and most vicious princes that occupied the Byzantine throne", was imprisoned and blinded. Blinding was one of the penalties for failure in that world. Yet even so it was more merciful than the torture and death that were often the fate of deposed emperors. It could be maintained that it was by his reluctance to kill his brother that the new Emperor, Alexius III, had provided the Doge and his nephew with an excuse for the present expedition. Isaac II, father of the Alexius who now accompanied Doge Dandolo towards Constantinople, had lain imprisoned in the imperial dungeons of Constantinople for eight years. The proclaimed object of the Doge was to restore his heir to the throne.

It was natural enough that a son should wish to take vengeance upon the man who had maimed his father and usurped his throne. Nevertheless, the young Alexius had no rightful grounds for his claim to the imperial mantle and the scarlet buskins of the Byzantine Emperor. Although in the later centuries of the Empire, and especially after the period of the powerful Macedonian dynasty, the children of the reigning sovereign had been regarded as more or less legitimate inheritors of the throne, the real tradition of Byzantium was inherited from ancient Rome. The Emperor was the heir of the Roman Caesars and, as such, he was in essence no more than *princeps* or first citizen.

It is true that there was no constitutional way of deposing an emperor once he was upon the throne, but recourse had always been had to the equally ancient Roman system of armed revolution, led by the subject most pleasing to the people.

"If the *coup* failed, he met with the shameful death of a usurper; if it succeeded, his victory was the sign that God's favour had abandoned the dethroned Emperor. Not a few emperors were forced to abdicate, or met a violent death as the result of revolts in camp or in the palace. Success legitimized the revolution. In a somewhat modified sense, Mommsen's description of the Principate—'the imperial power is an autocracy tempered by the legal right of revolution'—is applicable to the Byzantine Empire."*

Young Alexius had no legitimate claim upon the throne of Byzantium, and Doge Dandolo was certainly aware of this. His interest in Constantinople and its empire was realistic. Why should the Doge of Venice care about the legitimacy, or not, of the reigning Byzantine Emperor? The star of Venice had been rising for centuries, just as that of Byzantium had been declining. Pragmatic Venice was, in theory at any rate, the servant of the Roman Church, while the city founded by Constantine was the capital of the Orthodox Faith. Between these two branches of the Christian religion (which in those days was still strong enough to tolerate feud, division and strife between its members) a deep schism had long existed.

If the Doge wished to assuage his conscience for his contemplated attack on eastern Christendom, he need only remember that, in the eyes of the Pope, the Byzantines were heretics. It is always pleasant to be able to combine the necessary evils of business with the blessings of God.

The Doge, the Venetians and the Crusaders had already incurred the wrath of the Pope for their attack on the Christian city of Zara. For the violation of their crusading oaths they had incurred the very real and terrifying penalty of excommunication. Something of the thought that "It is better to be hung for a sheep than for a lamb" may have occurred to the Doge and to Boniface, the Marquis of Montferrat.

Enrico Dandolo, that patrician with the morals of a merchant on the make, was one of the ablest politicians of his day. He understood the nature and character of the Pope. Innocent III was one of the greatest popes in history, but as a great ruler and a man of affairs rather than as a spiritual authority. Unlike Dandolo, however, Innocent was no cynic. He was possessed by the belief that it was the will of God that the Pope should be supreme over all temporal rulers—even though this entailed his being increasingly devoted to mundane affairs. He genuinely regretted this involvement: "I have no leisure to meditate on supermundane things; scarce I can breathe. Yea, so much must I live for others, that almost I am a stranger to myself . . ." At the same time he made the claim (which he failed to see was at variance with Christ's "My Kingdom is not of this world") that "The Lord left to Peter the governance not of the Church only but of the whole world."

The supreme claim of the Papacy to dominion here on earth was made in the reply of Innocent III to the ambassadors of Philip Augustus of France when he had compelled that monarch to repudiate his wife Agnes and take back the wife whom, in the Pope's eyes, he had wrongfully divorced. Since this event had taken place in the year 1200, it is very possible that Dandolo knew of the Pope's statement. But whether he did or not, he certainly understood Innocent's view of the Papal position. "To princes power is given on earth, but to priests it is attributed also in heaven; to the former only of bodies, to the latter also over souls. Whence it follows that by so much as the soul is superior to the body, the priesthood is superior to the king-ship . . . Single rulers have single provinces, and single kings single kingdoms; but Peter, as in the plenitude, so in the extent of his power is pre-eminent over all, since he is the Vicar of Him whose is the earth and the fullness thereof, the whole wide world and all that dwell therein."

Dandolo had probably calculated that the submission of Constantinople to the arms of the crusaders would be justified if it entailed also the submission of the heretic Orthodox Eastern Church to the throne of Peter. If Dandolo could re-store to the true Faith the whole of the Byzantine Empire, spiritually at any rate, his act in taking that empire would be justified. If he could place upon the throne an emperor who owed his restoration to the force of crusading arms, that emperor would be willing to see that his church and his people accepted the spiritual jurisdiction of Rome. If at the same time this strengthened the Venetian trading position, even if it put into the hands of the Venetians and their allies all those rich terri-tories in eastern Europe, the Pope would surely be prepared to overlook the crime of making war upon fellow-Christians if it brought those Christians back to the Church of Rome. The young Alexius had already told Dandolo and the other leaders that "If God allows you to restore me to the throne, I will place all of my empire under obedience to Rome."

Other factors did undoubtedly contribute to the Crusaders' participation in this diversion from Egypt to Constantinople. Most important of all was the simple necessity to raise enough money to pay for the Venetian fleet that was transporting them. The leaders of the Crusade, who were in the confidence of the Doge (as far as that was ever given to any man), may well have been aware that the restoration of Alexius might not be possible, and that it might be necessary to capture Constantinople to secure the money they needed. The rank and file, however, as well as the main assembly of knights and nobility, knew only that Alexius had promised them 200,000 silver marks as a reward for restoring him to the throne. In addition to this, Alexius had guaranteed to victual the crusading army, and had stated that "If necessary I will personally go with you into the land of Babylon [Egypt], or, if you prefer it, I will send there at my own expense ten thousand men and maintain them there for a year."

His promise to submit the Orthodox Church to the Church of Rome might be of interest to the clergy, but to practical soldiers it was his financial and military aid that was appealing. Constantinople was a name to them and no more. They knew little or nothing of the ramifications of eastern trade which caused Venice to look upon her long-established rival as a deadly enemy. They had heard of Constantinople, as had nearly all citizens of western Europe in those centuries—the great Christian city at the end of the world, Mickle Garth, the Mighty Town—but it was more a legend than a reality. They knew nothing about the citizens of eastern Rome, nor what eastern Rome had meant to the world centuries before their own capitals, such as Paris and Brussels, were anything more than insignificant townships.

It was on June 23rd that the fleet finally came to anchor near the abbey of St. Stephen's, which lies about six miles south-west of Constantinople on the Sea of Marmora. It was a natural place to assemble before attempting the narrow fast-running strait of the Bosphorus. At such a distance the capital city of Constantine was little more than a shimmer of walls topped by towers. Even so, it was enough to cause the sophisticated Venetians to murmur with envy and admiration. Even the hardiest of the Crusaders understood at last the immensity of the enterprise upon which he had embarked. As Ville-hardouin wrote: "All those who had never seen Constantinople before gazed with astonishment at the city. They had never imagined that anywhere in the world there could be a city like this. They took careful note of the high walls and imposing towers that encircled it. They gazed with wonder at its rich palaces and mighty churches, for it was difficult for them to believe that there were indeed so many of them. As they gazed at the length and breadth of that superb city there was not a man, however brave and daring, who did not feel a shudder down his spine. One could not blame them, for never before in the whole history of the world had any men embarked upon so gigantic an enterprise . . ."

It was not true to say that the Crusaders were the first to attempt the fabulous walls and fortifications of Constantinople. Many armies and fleets before them had approached the 'God-guarded City' bent on its conquest. Not one of them had succeeded. Avars, Saracens and Bulgars had besieged the city. The Saracens had several times attacked it in the seventh century A.D., only to withdraw bloody and defeated from its walls. The Bulgars had twice laid siege to it, and did not relinquish their ambition until the great Emperor Basil II, the Bulgar-Slayer, put an end to the Bulgarian menace by sending 15,000 of their defeated army blinded, back to their homes. The Russians under Prince Igor had come down in a great fleet from the Black Sea in 1043 and had unwisely assailed the sea-ward walls. But then, as the chronicler described it, "liquid fire shot out upon our ships from long tubes placed in the parapets", so that the panic-stricken attackers later described how "The Greeks have a fire like the lightning of the skies. They cast it against us and burned us so that we could not conquer them . . ."

But the city was defended in the eyes of its inhabitants, not only by mechanical inventions and by its soldiers. Not for nothing was it known as the 'God-guarded City', for within its walls lay the True Cross on which Christ had been crucified, the drops of blood he had shed at Gethsemane and innumerable other relics of great power. They ranged from the stone on which Jacob had laid his head to sleep, the rod of Moses and the head of John the Baptist, to fragments and relics of almost every apostle and saint in the history of the Church.

As soon as the fleet had assembled in the anchorage off St. Stephen's Abbey, the Doge and the leaders of the Crusaders landed and held a conference. The Doge knew Constantinople better than any other member of the council. He had conducted a Venetian mission to the city over thirty years before, to sue for peace after the disasters that had befallen Venice in the war between the Republic and the Byzantine Empire. Dandolo had every reason to remember Constantinople, for it was during his stay within its walls that he had lost his eyesight. Whether this was due to a wound in the head (as Villehardouin asserts), to an illness, or—as was later maintained—to his being deliberately blinded by a burning-glass, the fact remains that the Doge had nourished an implacable hatred against the Byzantines ever since. His mission had proved unsuccessful, but his hatred of Constantinople was far deeper than any rancour that could possibly be due to a diplomatic failure. Under whatever circumstances the Doge had lost his eyesight, there seems little doubt that he held the city to blame. While the barons around him might be discussing the beauties of its towers and the formidable grandeur of its walls, Enrico Dandolo could only remember them—the colours of Santa Sophia, the green trees in the Emperor's gardens, the shipping on the Golden Horn and the multihued aspect of Byzantium.

His advice to the assembly was succinct. They should not attempt the city from overland, for the soldiers would scatter in search of food (of which they were already short), and the army would quickly disintegrate into a rabble. He told them that the solution lay across the Marmora, where the Princes' Islands shimmered under the sun, some ten miles away to the east. "There!" he said. "Those islands are inhabited by farmers. We can get corn and meat from them. Let us sail over and collect whatever provisions we need, and then proceed to take up our positions off the city. The fighting man who has a bellyfull of food acquits himself better than the man who is hungry."

But the following morning when the fleet weighed anchor, the wind had gone round to the south and was blowing straight up the Marmora. There could be no question of making for the Princes' Islands, so the ships took the wind under their sterns and made their way up the narrow strait towards the city. Now, for the first time, they could really see and appreciate the grandeur and immensity of its seaward walls. Although they were single walls and far simpler than the elaboration of ditches, double-walls and fortifications on the landward side, they rose sheer from the water. These seaward defences on the Marmora had been restored and strengthened by the Emperor

Theodosius in the fifth century. Although the subsequent misspending of Byzantine revenues by weak and indifferent emperors had failed to maintain them at their best, yet they still appeared unassailable. Furthermore, they had two important natural protections: the fast current which swept down the Bosphorus and which would render it almost impossible to beach a landing-craft and hold it in position while the troops got ashore; and the innumerable rocks and shoals which fringed the coastline and presented a dangerous hazard to any without expert local knowledge.

The day on which the Venetians and Crusaders sailed past the walls of Constantinople was dedicated in the Church Calendar to St. John the Baptist (whose head in its enamelled gold and gem-studded reliquary was one of the city's divine sources of protection). To honour the saint, the ships were dressed overall with banners and pennons, while every man entitled to a coat-of-arms had his shield displayed over the bulwarks. The Comte de Villehardouin was certainly under no illusion that the restoration of young Alexius was likely to be acceptable to the Byzantines, for he noted that "every man was assiduous in cleaning and preparing his arms and armour, for no one was in any doubt but that they would soon have need of them".

In order to assess the quality and nature of the defences, the fleet passed as close to the walls of the city as was consistent with safe navigation. If the Crusaders were concerned with examining the nature of their adversary, the inhabitants of Constantinople were no less interested to view the fleet. As far as they were concerned, Crusading armies had come through their territories before, and had never been anything other than a source of trouble. It had always needed immense diplomatic skill as well as payments of ready cash to get rid of them without open conflict. They had no reason to suspect that these Crusaders were bent on anything more than re-storing and re-victualling, although it may well have seemed curious to the more intelligent members of the populace that a Crusading army and fleet should have come so far north, if it was on its way to attack the Moslem kingdoms in the Levant and Egypt.

The sea-walls of Constantinople stretched from Acropolis

Point (modern Seraglio Point) to Studion near *Porta Aurea*, the Golden Gate. The men aboard the ships cannot have failed to remark this south-facing triple-entrance of marble, which stood only a quarter of a mile inland from the postern where the land walls of the city meet the sea. Built in imitation of the triumphal arches of ancient Rome, it was surmounted by a Cross, as befitted the New Rome where Christianity and the old Empire were allies.

Despite its crucifix, the gate was adorned with reliefs from classical mythology. It was through this gate that the Byzantine Emperors used to pass on their return from some victory in the field. Even here they managed to combine the memory of classical Rome with Christian Byzantium. They were dressed in the robes of the Caesars (though more gorgeous than any that the Roman Caesars had ever known) and they carried the sceptre of empire. Yet, as they passed through the Golden Gate, they were hailed by spectators who sang hymns of praise to God the Father, Giver of Victories.

As the ships worked their way up the strait, the inhabitants of the city crowded the battlements to watch them pass. "There were so many people on the walls," commented Villehardouin, "that it seemed as if there could be no more people left anywhere else in the world." Nobles and common soldiers, Frenchmen and Venetians alike, they gazed in awe at the majesty of a city which made even the largest in their own countries seem like villages. As they moved slowly to the north they passed the two small fortified harbours which were used by fishing-boats, and by shallow-draft merchantmen unable to round the Golden Horn on account of northerly winds. Eleven gates gave on to the sea between Studion and Acropolis Point, and the harbours of Eleutherius and Contoscalion were almost in the middle of the circuit. Although there had been no declaration or war, no word sent to the Emperor nor the people that they intended to place Alexius on the throne, no indication that they were other than friendly fellow-Christians, the Crusaders opened fire upon the anchored fishing-boats and merchantmen, showering them with arrows and the iron quarrels of crossbows.

Drawing level with the entrance of the Golden Horn, the

fleet turned slightly to the east in order to keep the wind astern. It directed its course towards the Asiatic shore, at this point only one mile distant. Behind the great chain that barred the entrance to the Golden Horn, the Mediterranean's finest natural harbour, they could see the lines of shipping at anchor and the shine of the white walls that guarded the city on its northern side. North of the Horn itself, the huddle of houses that constituted part of the international trading settlements, largely inhabited by Venetians and Genoese, climbed the steep slopes of Galata. In that quarter the invaders had many friends—merchants and ship-owners who owed their allegiance to Italy rather than Byzantium.

The size of the city and the vast extent of its walls and fortifications, the glistening towers of the palaces and the triumphal dome of Santa Sophia (the Cathedral of the Holy Wisdom) floating above the smoke haze, made an unforgettable sight. Robert de Clari, a French soldier who took part in the expedition, later remembered how "The people of Constantinople stood on the walls and the roofs of their houses to look at the marvel of the fleet. But the men in the ships regarded the grandeur of the city—so large it was and so long—and they were dumb with amazement."

2

CONSTANTINOPLE

"O CITY, city, queen of all cities!" exclaimed the Greek historian Ducas. "O city, heart of the four corners of the world! O Paradise planted in the west!" In his lament for a Constantinople that had for ever fled, he expressed something of the genuine reverence felt by all civilised men for this vast achievement in bricks, marble, stone and genius. It is difficult perhaps to comprehend in a century when the world is full of great cities, but explicable enough when one realises that in the Middle Ages Constantinople was the only capital known to Europeans that rivalled the glories of legendary Rome. It seemed like something left over from an age of giants. Within its walls there survived not only the memory of that great imperial past but also a rich and living culture that had grown, layer upon layer, ever since the even more distant days of Periclean Athens.

To most northerners, Constantinople was a dream not so far removed from Ultima Thule, the Golden Isles or the legendary land of Lyonnesse. So poor were communications, so difficult sea-passages, and so much had European civilisation declined since the collapse of the western Roman Empire, that the survival in the far east of Europe of a city which embraced an almost forgotten peak of human culture, and wedded it to the Christian tradition, seemed almost a miracle.

It was as if, in twentieth-century terms, the whole of Africa should revert to barbarism, and all its cities, roads and communications disappear. Yet at the same time a flourishing civilisation should still survive in the north, on the shores of the Mediterranean. At the heart of this civilisation there should

35

stand a brilliant Algiers, with universities and craftsmanship and an elegant, sophisticated way of life. With what amazement, then, would the inhabitants of a derelict town called Johannesburg, or a backward fishing-village called Durban, hear of a city that sounded like the legends they told round their camp-fires—of the giants who had once lived in the immense ruins surrounding their own squalid settlements? They would hear of buildings beyond their imagination, of fresh water that flowed into every house from inexhaustible cisterns, of great ships and golden palaces, and of people who dressed in silks and jewels. The cynics would scoff, the credulous would equate the story with some religious paradise, and the majority would listen with wonder—but with a complete lack of comprehension. Occasionally some merchants would return over thousands of miles of difficult and failing roadways, bringing with them artefacts and clothing, and objects carved in marble or ivory, or made of almost magical substances like glass. Then the dream would seem reality and the scoffers be silenced.

The city that rose in tier upon tier of houses, palaces, churches, shrines and markets on the banks of the Bosphorus was indeed a survivor from another world. The words which Walter Pater applied to the Mona Lisa might well have been used to describe Constantinople: "The presence that rose thus so strangely beside the waters is expressive of what in the ways of a thousand years men had come to desire . . . All the thoughts and experience of the world have etched and moulded there, in that which they have of power to refine and make expressive the outward form, the animalism of Greece, the lust of Rome, the mysticism of the middle age with its spiritual ambition and imaginative loves, the return of the Pagan world . . ." Constantinople was indeed a combination unique in history. It had kept alive the traditions and culture of the Greco-Roman civilisation for nine centuries, and had preserved the ethics and humanities of the Christian Faith against the attacks of innumerable barbarian invasions.

The influence of the city was spread far beyond the confines of those who had ever seen it, or even of those who had ever heard of it. Its artistic achievements alone, as Charles Diehl wrote,* made it sovereign: "In the cold fogs of Scandinavia and beside icy Russian rivers, in Venetian counting-houses or Western castles, in Christian France and Italy as well as in the Mussulman East, all through the ages folk dreamed of Byzantium, the incomparable city, radiant in a blaze of gold. As early as the sixth century the range of its influence was already astonishing, and its art had exercised a potent influence in North Africa, in Italy, and even in Spain. From the tenth to the twelfth centuries this influence became yet greater; Byzantine art was at that time 'the art which set the standard for Europe' . . . For any choice work, if it were difficult of execution or of rare quality, recourse was to be had to Constantinople. Russian princes of Kiev, Venetian doges, abbots of Monte Cassino, merchants of Amalfi, or Norman kings of Sicily— if a church had to be built, decorated with mosaics, or enriched with costly works in gold and silver, it was to the great city on the Bosphorus that they resorted for artists or works of art. Russia, Venice, southern Italy, and Sicily were at that time virtually provincial centres of East Christian art."

But it was not only for its works of art and its preservation of an ancient tradition of craftsmanship that the city was held in reverence. Here, within the walls of its libraries—both monastic and secular—were contained nearly all the wealth of literature surviving from the ancient world. The manuscripts of forever-lost plays by the great Greek dramatists, perhaps even the lyrics of Sappho, and an uncountable wealth of Greek and Roman authors—some of whose names we shall never know—these were housed in its libraries and given the same almost devout attention that was paid to the relics of the saints. Both were considered holy. If the word of the gods spoke through the manuscripts, the Word of God was evident in the wonder-working relics that were housed in miracles of gold and enamel.

Yet such a city could never be the perfection admired by some of its devotees in later centuries. It was human and, moreover, it stood at the confluence of the East and the West, where not only the virtues but also the vices of both natures were equally mingled. The Byzantium imagined by W. B. Yeats possibly existed:

> *... such a form as Grecian goldsmiths make*
> *Of hammered gold and gold enamelling*
> *To keep a drowsy Emperor awake;*
> *Or set upon a golden bough to sing*
> *To lords and ladies of Byzantium*
> *Of what is past, or passing, or to come.**

There was another Byzantium. It was recorded by travellers and ambassadors who visited it during these centuries, as well as by its own native historians. "The eunuchs who preserve the mountains and the forests for the emperor's hunting with as much care as the ancient pagans guarded the groves sacred to their gods (or with a fidelity like that of the angel who guards the gates of Paradise) were ready to kill any one who even tried to cut timber for the fleet."* That, in itself, helps to explain why the ships of Byzantium were not ready in their hundreds to oppose the invader.

Of the blinded Isaac, whose son was now preparing to besiege Constantinople, Nicetas Choniates, the contemporary Greek historian, wrote that: "Forests of game, seas of fishes, rivers of wine, and mountains of bread went to make his daily table." Isaac, if one may trust this historian (who was a deeply religious conservative, in love with a lost golden age), was never happy to appear in the same robes on more than one day, and spent a great deal of time at the steam baths (that inheritance from Rome, now called 'Turkish'). "He went about glorious as a peacock," wrote Sir Edwin Pears, echoing in Victorian sentiment the moral strictness of his Byzantine predecessor. "(He) was fond of songs, and his gates were ever open to actors, buffoons, and jugglers."

It is true that the later emperors had misspent their fabulous inheritance, but if Byzantium was decadent it was due more to the ceaseless blood-letting of centuries of warfare than to the profligate excesses of weak rulers. The city which had stood inviolate on the shores of the Bosphorus for hundreds of years had not achieved its pre-eminent position by accident.

Older by far than the religion it now proclaimed, the city of Byzantium had been founded in 657 B.C. by Greek colonists who had wisely appreciated its superb position and the easy dominance that this gave over the Euxine grain trade. Although the narrow channel of the Dardanelles to the south might have seemed an equally good place to found a city with the intention of controlling the all-important trade-route between Russia, the Black Sea and the civilisations of the Mediterranean, the particular advantage of the narrow Bosphorus was that it was the main crossing-point between Europe and Asia for the over-land caravan routes. Byzantium stood not only at the gates to the Black Sea and to the important Russian grain-trade, it was also the meeting-point of the main trade-route between the continents of Europe and Asia. It commanded these two all-important sources of wealth in the ancient world.

Byzantium did not play a significant part in the history of the classical period, largely because it was so far to the north. Geographically it was outside the mainstreams both of culture and of conflict. As communications improved, and as the bias of the Roman world moved increasingly to the East, so it was inevitable that what had once been no more than an important trading centre should take on a more prominent role.

Quite apart from its attractive and defensible situation on a promontory of seven hills, the city was blessed by something unusual in the Mediterranean—a deep-water bay that stretched some seven miles into the land. It was, indeed, this geographical accident that, more than anything else, led to the development of the great city. This unique natural harbour was known from its shape, from the richness of the city that it fostered, from the innumerable fish that thronged its waters, and from the press of shipping that gathered there, as the Golden Horn.

If there was any disadvantage to the city of Byzantium, it was to be found in its climate. A modern traveller* has aptly observed that its main drawback is "the damp that rises from the three seas; on summer evenings, when the heat makes it intolerable to sit indoors, the damp makes it intolerable to sit out of doors, whether one suffers the miasma of the Golden Horn as one watches the waxing moon over Stamboul from the Rue des Petits Champs or thereabouts, or the miasma of the Bosphorus as one watches the waning moon over Asia from

Taxim or one of the garden-restaurants below it. Only the islands are free from this, and they are far away. Another physical trial is the wind that blows down from the Black Sea and, swirling round street-corners, puffs finely powdered dung in your face . . ."

Worse than the lethargic humidity of summer are the northerly winds which in spring and winter blow down from the Black Sea. With all of frozen Russia on their wings, they blast the city with snow and turn its marble columns into monuments of despair. The climate, then, was probably one reason why both Greeks and Romans tended to ignore Byzantium's potentials. As a residential city they were prepared to leave it to the coarse fibres of merchants and trading captains.

As an important economic centre Byzantium played its part in the history of the ancient world, but it did not achieve any great cultural or political significance until the fourth century A.D. During the struggle for the Roman Empire between Constantine and his brother-in-law Licinius, the latter used Byzantium as his main base, for he had observed that it was upon this city that the whole eastern empire of Rome pivoted. Constantine did not fail to notice this either, and upon his defeating Licinius and becoming emperor of both the eastern and western hemispheres, he decided that a new capital was needed. This was not a decision based upon any *folie de grandeur* nor was it based upon religious prejudice against pagan Rome (Constantine was no Ikhnaton), for the need had long been felt for a new heart to the Roman Empire.

From a practical point of view, Rome was too far removed from the frontiers that were now of prime importance—the Danube and the Asian front stretching from Armenia to Syria. It was here in the North and the East that the main threat to the stability of the Mediterranean world now came. Byzantium was ideally suited to be garrison, naval base and administrative centre, for it was almost equidistant between the two sources of danger. Rome, in the eyes of the later emperors, also carried with it the dead weight of its old republican attachments. It was, in any case, uncongenial to rulers whose interest lay increasingly in the East. Constantine himself had been born at

Naissus (Nish in modern Jugoslavia), and at one time had considered founding a new capital in his birthplace.

The Emperor had perhaps another reason for wishing to found a capital city that would be free of many of the attachments of ancient Rome—he had been converted to Christianity by a conspicuous miracle. This was the famous 'Vision of the Flaming Cross', which had appeared to him in the sky one day at high noon, accompanied by the words 'By this, conquer', Constantine, therefore, wished to found a Christian city, and it so happened that Byzantium fulfilled all his requirements. It possessed an almost unassailable position, commanded the most important trade-routes, and it appealed to his own desire for a capital in the East. All these things combined to suggest that God himself had elected Byzantium as the capital of a Christian Roman Empire.

Although the victorious Emperor renamed the city 'New Rome', it was always known in his memory as Constantinople, the City of Constantine. Its ancient name Byzantium—far from being totally dispossessed—lingered on to embrace an empire, a way of life and a culture, so that 'Byzantine' to this day may indicate the design of a church in Russia or Syria, a style of painting, or a hair-fine mode of definition in religious or political argument. A number of English writers, most notably the great historian Edward Gibbon, have contrived to give the adjective 'Byzantine' a pejorative sense. This must be largely ascribed to an Anglo-Saxon inability to comprehend the finer shades of aesthetic and political definition, let along the nuances of religious interpretation. The shades of Byzantium, whose empire lasted for a thousand years and whose influence upon the world is still far from exhausted, need not be disturbed.

The city founded by Constantine was completed in less than six years, and was inaugurated by the Emperor in May A.D. 330. In the centuries that followed, it became not only the capital of the Roman Empire but the only truly civilised city in Europe. When Rome fell to its northern invaders, and when the whole of the western empire gradually dissolved (to become a mass of petty and backward states), at the end of the Mediterranean there shone the New Rome. Enriched by the whole of the great classical past, it comprised the imperial functions that had once been those of Rome, the legacy of Athens and of Greek culture, and the patina of the Hellenistic civilisation which had graced cosmopolitan Alexandria (until extinguished by the Arabic conquest).

The Emperor Alexius III, who now watched the fleet of the Crusaders as it passed the mouth of the Golden Horn and turned East towards the Asiatic shore, was among the most contemptible in the history of this great city and empire. Less vicious than some of his predecessors, he suffered from the greatest disadvantage of those who inherit great wealth and power—he "was under the impression that work was inconsistent with the dignity of an emperor".* Whatever might be held against Doge Dandolo, he at least had always been aware that great things are not achieved by little effort. The Doge knew that the power and the glory belong to those who have the capacity to rule the world, and not be ruled by it.

3

THE FIRST SKIRMISH

THE Crusaders' first requirement was to get the troops fed, and the fleet victualled and watered. Since it was now harvesttime, the fertile land on the Asiatic shore opposite the city was the obvious place to disembark. There was, furthermore, a small harbour at Chalcedon, opposite Constantinople, where the fleet could safely anchor.

The night of June 24th saw the eastern coastline of the Bosphorus dense with sails and shipping. Their lights sparkled across the water, and on the shore the camp-fires of the Crusaders glowed against the dark land-mass of Asia. The city shone brighter than any that the Crusaders had seen before—torches passing along the battlemented walls, the glitter of the great houses and the diamond-brilliance of Blachernae, the imperial palace fronting on to the Golden Horn. Santa Sophia floated above Acropolis Point like a luminous bubble. For centuries the oil lamps under its fabulous dome had gleamed through the arches supporting it, acting as a pharos to ships outward or homeward bound.

The Doge and the leaders of the barons took over one of the Byzantine Emperor's summer palaces in Chalcedon. The others had their tents and pavilions brought out from the ships and set up in the town or on its outskirts. As Villehardouin tells us: "The horses were now disembarked and all the knights and sergeants landed in full armour, leaving no one aboard the ships except the sailors. The land around was beautiful and fruitful; heaps of cut corn which had just been reaped were stacked in the fields so that anyone in need could take as much as he wanted . . ."

43

Two days later, having plundered Chalcedon, the fleet moved a mile to the north. It rounded Damalis (Leander's Tower) and came to anchor in the well-protected harbour of Chrysopolis (modern Üsküdar). The Crusaders and the Venetians moved up and encamped around Chrysopolis, the leaders taking possession of another of the Emperor's summer palaces. Meanwhile the troops ransacked the coastal plain.

Whatever reports may by now have reached the Emperor from spies or well-wishers in Corfu as to the aims and intentions of the Crusaders, he can have been in little doubt that they would cost his city and his country a considerable amount before they could be sent on their way. He may have believed, as had happened with other Crusading armies in the past, that they would peaceably withdraw if presented with a large enough bribe. Crusaders were always short of money—that indeed was the reason why many of them had left their homes in the first place. "There were some trifling temporal advantages," wrote an ironic commentator, "attending the crusades: Pope Innocent declares that the goods of the Crusaders are under the protection of Saint Peter, and therefore freed from taxes and impositions; also that if the Crusaders be in debt, Christian creditors are to be compelled by the spiritual courts, and Jews by the temporal sword, to remit the payment of interest. If a crusade upon such terms were now to be proclaimed!"*

Those who 'took the Cross' were not always noble citizens impelled by a heaven-sent spirit of duty to fight against the enemies of Christ's Church. As often as not, they were seedy nobility with insufficient land to produce a suitable standard of living; malefactors who had been ordered by their confessors to make the journey in expiation of their sins; debtors eager to escape the unpleasant fate (such as an oar-bench at the galleys) which was their lot in those days; and unemployed soldiers ever ready to turn a dishonest penny in the wake of a sanctified cause.

All this the Emperor knew, for whatever his weakness and his criminal neglect of his charge, he was still a native of Byzantium. He knew as well as any of his subjects that the Crusaders were not saints in arms. Accordingly, Alexius III ordered the army to march out of the city and take up their stations on the shore opposite the Crusaders' encampment at Chrysopolis. His intention was to oppose any attempt at landing north of the Golden Horn near the suburb of Galata. He despatched his most important officer to the Asian coastline, to maintain a watch over the invaders. This was his brother-in-law, Michael Stryphnos, who held the curious title of *Megas Dux* (a Byzantine amalgam in that *Megas* is Greek for 'Great', and *Dux* Latin for 'Leader'). He was also known as *Strategos of the Carabisiani*, or General of the Caraboi (a type of warship)—in modern terms, Admiral of the Fleet.

Unfortunately, under the disastrous rule of the Emperor Alexius III, the title had become almost meaningless. This was why Michael Stryphnos, instead of cutting the Venetian fleet to pieces where it lay at anchor off Scutari, was now in command of 500 Greek cavalry. Nicetas says of Stryphnos that "he had sold the anchors, sails, and everything else belonging to the Byzantine navy which could possibly be turned into money". It seems more than likely, for it was only the known weakness of the Byzantine fleet that had made Doge Dandolo confident of his ability to land an army on these shores. The fleet which had dominated the Mediterranean for centuries and had turned back innumerable invaders from the city was non-existent. The fleet from which Venice had learned the art of galley-fighting now rotted helpless behind the barrier of the Golden Horn. Meanwhile, its Admiral led a troop of horsemen as ineffectual scouts on the flanks of the Fourth Crusade.

Even as a cavalry leader Michael Stryphnos did not distinguish himself. When attacked by about eighty mounted knights (led by four French noblemen) he and his men turned and fled. It was the first encounter between the Crusaders and the Byzantine army and it marked the beginning of open conflict.

Whatever one may feel about the behaviour of the Greek cavalry, one thing must be borne in mind—war had not yet been declared. As far as Michael Stryphnos and his troops were concerned, no reason had been given as to why the Crusaders and their Venetian allies were in the Sea of Marmora, let alone why they were threatening the dominions of fellow-Christians.

In the twentieth century, wars begin whenever a suitable opportunity occurs for the aggressor, but this was the so-called 'Age of Chivalry'—not the age of cynicism. Even a private conflict did not start without a formal exchange between the opponents, while wars between nations were usually the subject of complicated formalities, and an announcement of intention so clear as to preclude any possibility of surprise attack. (Even as late as the sixteenth century when the Spanish Armada met the English fleet in the Channel, Admiral Howard 'proclaimed war' by sending his admiral's pinnace over to the Spanish Admiral, while the latter hoisted a consecrated banner to his main-top to indicate that he accepted Howard's challenge.) The behaviour, then, of the Fourth Crusade in invading Christian territory without any announcement of its intentions, and without any pretext or reason, must be considered one of the most despicable acts in the history of 'Christian' nations. It was the breakdown of a theory, however fallacious this may have been, that peoples professing Christianity were united against an outside world which was hostile to its tenets. It was two and a half centuries before Niccolò Machiavelli would found the science of modern politics by "ascribing all things to natural causes or to fortune", yet his concepts were certainly similar to those of Doge Dandolo. (It often takes men of letters a long time to formulate the conclusions that have been practised for centuries by those whose business lies in the government of the world.)

That small incident over 700 years ago—the attack on the Byzantine cavalry by the Crusaders—foreshadows the events of our own sad century. For a short time in the history of the world it had been proclaimed (even if not believed) that "might is not right". From now on, the pattern of politics was to alter:

> All changed, changed utterly:
> A terrible beauty is born.*

If Christians might attack fellow-Christians without excuse or justification—but with only an eye to the main chance and to material advantage—then the creed which Rome had adopted was clearly quite different from the one that had been formulated by its Founder.

Throughout its troubled centuries of incessant warfare, the Orthodox Church of the East had been engaged against pagans or against the self-proclaimed enemies of Christianity. They had had to barter, connive and often make opportunist 'deals' with these enemies, in order to preserve their own life. Their aim, nevertheless, had been to establish the Christian Church and the traditions of the Roman Empire over barbarians, or over those whom they held to be the followers of a mistaken and evil faith. Even their conflicts on previous occasions with Normans or Venetians or Crusading armies, had been dictated not by any desire to win land from these westerners but solely in defence of their own territories and sphere of influence. It was left to western Europe, and in particular to Venice and France, to prove to Byzantium that its real enemies were fellow-Christians.

After this first clash of arms, the Crusaders felt confident in their superiority. "With the help of God the engagement was brief and successful, for the Greeks fled, our troops pursuing them for all of a league. We then seized a good number of horses, palfreys, mules, tents, and other booty . . ."* The next day an ambassador came over to Scutari from Constantinople. He was Nicholas Roux, a Lombard who had been selected for his post because he could speak the language of the invaders. He had been sent, as he immediately explained, to find out why the Crusaders were occupying and pillaging Byzantine territory.

"You are Christians, and so is the Emperor. He is well aware that you are on your way to the Holy Land, to deliver the holy places from the infidel. He wonders, therefore, why you have come into his country. If you are in want and short of supplies, he will readily give you food and money—but on condition that you leave his territory. He is more than unwilling to do you any harm, though he is perfectly capable of it—as you must well know—if you refuse to go on your way."

Conon de Béthune, one of the more cultured knights (he was something of a poet and an orator), was chosen to reply. He

maintained that the Crusaders had not invaded the lands of
Alexius III, since they were not his. "They belong," he said,
"to his nephew, and he is here with us. But, if your master is
willing to throw himself on his nephew's mercy and restore to
him his crown and throne, we will intercede with the young
prince to forgive his uncle and allow him enough money to live
upon in luxury." He concluded by saying that unless the
messenger returned with an acceptance of these conditions he
had better not come back at all.

For the first time, the purpose of the Crusaders was made
brutally clear to the Emperor and his people. It was unlikely
that Alexius III would respond to this message, with its specious
explanation of the Crusaders' presence in his lands, and with
its suspect promise that his security would be assured. It left
him with no option but to abdicate, or to trust that the army
and the citizens would support him against the invaders.

There can be little doubt that young Alexius had managed
to convince the barons that he was assured of popular support
in the city. Like many another exile and pretender, he was
probably under the illusion that his name would evoke an
immediate response in the people. He may well have believed
that they would respond to his appeal, dethrone his uncle and
open the gates to their liberators.

The council of the Doge and the barons certainly acted as
if they thought that the sight of Alexius would be sufficient to
induce a popular revolt in his favour. It is likely that the barons
did indeed believe this, although it is hardly credible that the
Doge (with his excellent espionage system in the City) could
have been so duped. For the people of Constantinople,
however much they may have disliked their slothful and
sybaritic emperor, were certain to resent having another and
unknown ruler forced upon them by an army of foreigners.
Their reaction was perfectly understandable—if Alexius III
was to be deposed, they themselves would have the rightful
say as to who should be his successor.

The day after the despatch of their message to the Emperor,
ten galleys embarked the Doge, the Pretender Alexius, and the
senior knights, and rowed them over to Acropolis Point.

According to Robert de Clari, the Doge had suggested that they should show Alexius to the people of the city—in the hope that this would evoke a wave of popular feeling for him, and that the Byzantines themselves would accomplish the object of the expedition. The galleys passed as close to the walls as they dared, while Alexius was 'showed' to his people. A herald cried out that this was their rightful ruler, and that it was their duty to rally to his side. "But if you do not acknowledge him," the herald concluded, "we will reduce you to utter ruin!"

Ever eager to put a good face on the Crusaders' actions and to justify them in the eyes of posterity, Villehardouin maintained that the Byzantines did not dare show themselves to be on the side of young Alexius 'out of their fear and terror of the Emperor'. Robert de Clari's account, however, is far more convincing. It reveals a reaction quite consistent with the nature of a proud people when faced with the demands of insolent foreigners.

"He is not our emperor!" they cried from the walls. "We have never heard of him!"

Alexius's credentials were again recited to the crowd, and yet again they shouted back, "We have never heard of him!"

Whatever the Doge's feelings may have been at this response, there is no doubt that the knights now realised—many of them for the first time—that they were faced with a siege. It would be a siege, moreover, of the largest city in Europe; a city that had never been taken by an enemy; and whose defences had always been regarded as impregnable. It says something for their resolution and courage that they appear to have accepted this challenge without hesitation. If there had been any left who disliked the idea of making war upon fellow-Christians, now would have been the time for them to declare themselves. It seems, however, as if there were no dissentients to the proposed assault on 'the God-guarded City'.

"Next morning, after attending mass, the barons gathered on horseback for a council in the open fields . . ." After a lengthy 'parliament', the command of the various divisions of the army was settled. Baldwin, Count of Flanders, was to lead the advance guard—largely because he had among his followers a great number of trained soldiers, archers and crossbowmen. The second division was led by his brother; the third by the Count of Saint Paul; the fourth by Count Louis de Blois; the fifth (which included the chronicler Villehardouin) by Matthew de Montmorency; the sixth was composed of knights and soldiers from Burgundy; and the rearguard was led by the Marquis of Montferrat.

Except for this rearguard, which was a mixture of Italians and Germans, almost the entire composition of the invading army was Norman–French or French tributaries. The French were more responsible than any others for the events that were to follow. Almost certainly they were the dupes of the Venetians, but it was they who provided the arms and the men without which the attack on Constantinople would have been impossible.

4

MACHINATIONS IN VENICE

THE Crusaders who were now preparing to invest Constantinople had taken a long time to reach this corner of the earth, so remote from their original intention. If Innocent III was its moving spirit, the Fourth Crusade had been launched in France several years before and was a lay enterprise from its very beginning. In 1199 a group of French knights had discussed the possibility of a new Crusade at the castle of Count Tibald of Champagne. Inspired by an itinerant preacher, Fulk of Neuilly, they had decided to 'take the Cross', and had immediately sent a message to the Pope announcing their intention.

Innocent III had proclaimed his desire for a new Crusade to free the Holy Land immediately upon ascending the pontifical throne. It was with pleasure, then, that he heard this news from Champagne. Although, throughout the course of his long and successful pontificate, Innocent III made every effort to revive the ancient spirit of the Crusades (made it indeed his supreme goal), he failed utterly in this ambition. His great desire was to re-establish the papal control of the Crusades, and from the very inception of the Fourth it was clear that the French had taken matters into their own hands. Having chosen their own leader they then decided their route and their objective without even consulting the Pope.*

Negotiations and preparations for the Crusade went on throughout the year 1200, but in 1201 the chosen leader, Tibald of Champagne, unexpectedly died. This led to a further delay, which was only resolved when Boniface, Marquis of Montferrat, was selected to take his place. This news cannot have been pleasing to the Pope, for the Lombard House of

Montferrat was a close ally of the Hohenstaufen (those enemies
of Papal power and, incidentally, of Byzantium). All the same,
the choice cannot have been unforeseen by the Pope, for the
Montferrats had notable connections with the Crusades and
with the East.

In the summer of 1201 Boniface left his territories in northern
Italy and visited France to confer with the French leaders, and
to receive his formal appointment at their hands. Well aware
that it was his Hohenstaufen connections which made him
acceptable in French eyes, he wasted no time in demonstrating
that these were still potent. After leaving France, he went
north to Germany and spent several months with Philip of
Swabia, who was anticipating that he would soon become
Emperor of the West.

The dislike felt by Philip of Swabia for Byzantium and especially for its present ruler was no secret. It was inherited from
his ancestors, and particularly from his brother, Henry VI, who,
had been on the very point of launching an attack on Constantinople when he had died at Messina in 1197. Furthermore,
Philip had strong personal reasons for wishing to see the present
Emperor of Byzantium, Alexius III, removed from the throne.
Philip was married to Irene Angelina, the daughter of the
dethroned and blinded Isaac, and his marriage (unusual in
those days for rulers) was a genuine love-match. The fate of his
father-in-law, then, was very much a matter of personal concern to Philip. It was during those winter months which Boniface of Montferrat passed in close consultation with Philip of
Swabia that something akin to a plot against the Byzantine
Empire was hatched. From now on, one may begin to trace a
sinister and deliberate misdirection of the Fourth Crusade.

But even if Boniface and Philip had agreed together that a
subsidiary aim of the Crusade should be to dethrone Alexius
III and restore the dynasty of Isaac Angelus, it would still have
been extremely difficult—indeed almost impossible—to achieve,
without some extraordinary justification. It was at this moment
that the instrument for their design was most opportunely
delivered to their hands. The young Alexius, Isaac Angelus's
son, escaped from Constantinople to Sicily and made his way

from there to the Swabian court. This was natural enough
since his sister was the beloved wife of Swabia's ruler. Alexius,
in fact, had got away from Constantinople during the summer,
and it is just possible that Philip of Swabia knew that his arrival
was imminent when he invited Boniface to visit him.

If Philip needed a plausible excuse for the proposed diversion
of the Fourth Crusade, and if Boniface was equally ready to
use his position as its leader to misdirect it, both of them now
had their wants supplied. It is still doubtful whether an attack
on Constantinople can, at this moment, have been any more
than a desirable but somewhat speculative scheme. Boniface
and Philip knew that most of the knights and men-at-arms who
would embark on the Crusade would never consider any idea
of turning aside to attack Christian territory. They had an
instrument in Alexius—no more—and they now needed a
really valid reason to use him.

In February 1201, prior to the death of Tibald of Champagne
and the appointment of Boniface to succeed him, six ambassadors had arrived in Venice from France empowered to treat
with the Doge on the subject of transport for the Crusade.
Venice had not been their first port of call, for they had previously been to both Genoa and Pisa, only to be told that
the Genoese were unwilling, and the Pisans unable, to provide
them with transport. It was for this reason, as Robert de Clari
tells us, that they finally made the journey to Venice (they had
probably hoped for better terms from the Genoese and Pisans).
The ambassadors put their proposition to the Doge and his
council who, after a week of discussion, agreed to transport the
Crusaders at a price of five marks per horse, and two marks
per man. According to Villehardouin who, as one of the leaders,
was in a good position to know the figures, the Crusaders
numbered 4,000 knights, each with his horses, 9,000 squires
and 20,000 foot soldiers.* For the sum of 86,000 marks the
Venetians agreed to carry the men and horses "to recapture
Jerusalem," and to victual them for a year. In addition, the
Venetians said that they would "for the love of God" provide
fifty armed galleys as escort, on condition that they should have
half of any conquests that might be made. If the Crusade was

to proceed, the ambassadors could do nothing but accept these terms. Nowhere else in Europe could they hope to find a maritime power capable of supplying them with the fleet that they needed.

Pope Innocent III was now acquainted with the terms of the contract. It was one to which he very reluctantly acceded. He had little reason to trust the Venetians, for he knew that they would transport anyone—Christian or Moslem—for a fee. As if well aware of the possibilities latent behind the present agreement, he inserted a clause to the effect that no Christian state must on any account be attacked and that, to ensure this, a papal legate must sail with the fleet. It is likely that he suspected Doge Dandolo of some design against Zara, but unlikely that he ever anticipated an attack on Constantinople. Subject to these conditions, then, it was understood by the Pope and by the Crusaders that the Venetian fleet would be transporting the army to Alexandria in Egypt.

There were very good reasons for attacking Egypt. Once the port of Alexandria had been taken, it would be comparatively easy to keep the army supplied and reinforced by the sea-route from Europe. The old Crusader route across the Dardanelles and down through Asia Minor to Syria had become increasingly dangerous owing to the mounting power of the Turks, who were in the process of absorbing all of Anatolia. In the Third Crusade, the magnificent German army under Frederick I, Emperor of the West, had been bled to death in battle after battle against the Turks. When it finally won through to Acre no more than 1,000 men remained.

Egypt at this moment was weakened by a recent civil war. The Nile had failed to inundate the land for five whole years, with the result that the Egyptians were starving, and their morale had collapsed. Egypt, nevertheless, was the mainstay of Arabic wealth and if it could be captured, a wedge would be driven between the Moslem world to the east and the western territories of North Africa. There was every good reason, then, why the Crusaders should decide on Egypt as the target for their expedition. Once they had established their base and headquarters in Egypt, they could keep a steady transfusion of men and *matériel* flowing in from their native countries. At the same time they themselves could live off the land of Egypt—for the Nile would not consistently fail and even if the Egyptians starved there would always be plenty of grain and other supplies sufficient for a relatively small Crusading army.

One thing the Crusaders did not know was that, while they were conducting negotiations with the Venetians for their transport, the Venetians were in Cairo, possibly concluding what amounted to a non-aggression pact with the Egyptians.*

In the spring of 1202, just over a year before the Crusade reached Byzantine territory and prepared to attack Constantinople, the Venetians were negotiating a trade agreement with al-Adil, Sultan of Egypt. The advantage of this agreement to Venice was immense, and it was largely upon it that so much of the city's later fortune was founded. In return for a guarantee by the Venetians that they would prevent any Crusading army from attacking Egypt, the Sultan guaranteed them considerable trading concessions in Alexandria.

Egypt, with its outlet to the Red Sea and to the merchandise of India and the East, was in a position to control the flow to Europe not only of oriental luxuries but also of those spices upon which the preservation and enhancement of European food so largely depended during the winter months. It was unlikely, if they had concluded a trading agreement of such importance with the Sultan of Egypt, that the Venetians would willingly have countenanced any attack upon the Sultan's domains. The chronicler Ernoul, or Arnold of Ibelino (who would have had no reason to invent such a story) states specifically that the Sultan "sent envoys to Venice and told the Venetians that, if they could prevent the Christians attacking his country, he would give them ample reward . . ." Ernoul further goes on to say that "He wished the Doge and the Venetians both health and friendship—and to prove it sent them a great variety of presents. He further guaranteed that, if they could prevent the Franks [the Crusaders] from attacking Egypt, he would pay them a considerable sum and would ensure that they had very advantageous trading concessions at the port of Alexandria."*

There is no longer any great mystery about the diversion of the Fourth Crusade, once one has seen how very much Venice stood to gain by preventing the Crusaders from ever reaching its objective. When this is coupled with the fact that the leader of the Crusade, Boniface of Montferrat, was in agreement with Philip of Swabia to divert the Crusade to Constantinople if it were at all possible—then the pattern of events becomes immediately clear.

Not all the Crusaders were willing to wait while the negotiations over transport were settled with Venice. A Flemish squadron under John of Nesle sailed and reached Acre in the winter of 1202, while yet another group set out independently from Marseilles. Some individuals even made their own charter arrangements, rather than wait for the main body of the Crusade to assemble. Nevertheless, these independent groups were only a fraction of the great army that was gathering throughout Europe—and which was to be dependent solely upon Venice for its transport to the Near East. Most of the Crusaders did not even know that Egypt had been decided upon by their leaders as the main point of attack. A great many of them believed that Syria was to be the objective. Some of them disagreed violently in the choice of Egypt, and tried to make their own way to Syria. It was these latter whom Villehardouin so harshly castigated as having splintered the Crusade. Certainly, the 'pro-Syria' party was the cause of many of the arguments and dissension that broke out when the army was finally encamped at Venice.

So, gradually throughout the years 1202-3, the majority of the Crusaders and men-at-arms made their way through Europe, most of them taking the route over the Alps by Mont Cenis, and across Lombardy to Venice. It was the failure of many of the knights to arrive at Venice on time, or to make their own arrangements and sail from other ports of embarkation, which caused grave concern to the leaders of the Crusade. They realised that they would be unable to fulfil their promises to the Venetians as to the number of men and horses that would need transport, and they would therefore be unable to pay the sum that had been agreed. Since they had borrowed 5,000 silver marks from Venetian money-lenders on their first visit to the city—so that the boat-builders could begin their work—they were now in a similar position to a shipping company that has begun to build a 40,000-ton liner and suddenly realises that a 10,000-ton vessel would have been big enough.

It was hardly surprising that men like Villehardouin became embittered against the groups of knights who had already sailed from Flanders, or who were now making their own private arrangements in other ports of Europe. Villehardouin himself, in company with a number of other senior knights, was despatched to induce some of the reluctant, or independent-minded, Crusaders to come to Venice. Villehardouin, for instance, was successful in persuading Count Louis de Blois to join up with the main body and not proceed independently.

While Villehardouin and other members of the inner council were increasingly concerned at the situation in which they found themselves, a simple Crusader like Robert de Clari could only marvel at the sight of the fleet that was in preparation: "When the Crusaders were all assembled at Venice and saw the great fleet which had been built—the fine merchantmen, warships, transports to carry the horses, and the galleys, they were amazed —almost as much as they were at the great richness of the city. Now when they saw that there was not room for them all in Venice, they decided to go and encamp on the island of Saint Nicholas, which is a league from Venice and entirely surrounded by sea . . ."

It was at this point that their troubles really started. Nothing could have pleased the Doge more than that the bulk of the Crusading army should be located in one place, and cut off from his city. He had no more desire to have this host of soldiers quartered in Venice itself than have many other rulers in subsequent centuries who have seen 'armies of liberation' descending upon their capitals. But now, as Villehardouin records, "The Venetians had faithfully fulfilled their part of the bargain—indeed they had built more ships than was necessary. So, being ready to start, they asked the counts and barons to fulfil their part of the bargain and pay the money that was owing."

A great number of the Crusaders had run out of funds and in their turn looked to the senior knights to help them. "The barons accordingly took from each man as much as he could afford to pay. But even so, after everyone had made some contribution or other, the total sum collected from the army did not amount to half—let alone the whole—of the sum that had been agreed upon."

Doge Dandolo was one of the most astute men of his age. It is difficult to believe that he had not always foreseen that something of this sort was likely to occur. Venice had been familiar with Crusaders and their financial problems for two centuries. Not only were there always defections from their ranks, individuals who decided at the last moment to make their own arrangements, but the average crusader—particularly the common man-at-arms—was invariably short of money. As the Doge knew, this was one of the reasons that may well have driven him to join the Crusade in the first place. Certainly all Crusaders hoped to recoup their expenditure—and make a profit during the campaign itself. Was it by chance, then, that the Venetians appear to have built many more ships than were ever likely to have been required? There was "So great a number of warships, galleys and transports that they could well have accommodated three times as many men as there were in the whole army".

In the discussions that followed among the barons, there were many who were in favour of abandoning the idea of a centralised expedition, and of making their way individually to Egypt or Syria. Naturally their leaders were against any such notion, for to disband the Crusading army would be to render any major attack on Egypt an impossibility. The leaders borrowed all that they could, and prevailed on their followers to do the same. At the same time they even had their private plate sent over to the Doge in lieu of money. "It was a wonderful sight to see the gold and silver table-services being carried to the Doge's palace to make up the money due." But it was to no avail, for even after the barons and lesser nobility had scraped together all that they could, they still remained 34,000 marks short of the sum that had originally been promised.*

Doge Dandolo could afford the luxury of a smile. He had the bulk of the Crusading army safely settled on the island of Saint Nicholas, where they could be supplied by boat—but only at his convenience. A large percentage of the money that had just been paid to him had actually been borrowed at high rates in Venice, thus giving the local money-lenders an enviable hold over the borrowers. At a conservative estimate the Doge of Venice had some 50,000 marks in the exchequer. (It is difficult to calculate the exact sum, since part of it had been paid in gold and silver plate.) He had immensely increased the sea-power of the Republic in galleys, merchantmen and transports, by putting all the local shipyards to work on the Crusaders' commission. All the ships, which would in any case be Venetian-manned, would revert to the Republic on the conclusion of the campaign. Furthermore, he was now in the position—as he explained to the Council—to retain both money and ships unless the Crusaders could complete their part of the bargain.

"These people are unable," he said, "to pay us any more. They are unable to keep the agreement they have made with us. So we for our part are fully entitled to retain the money that they have already paid us. No civilised state in the world would deny us our right to behave in this way. Neither we nor Venice would be blamed if that was what we did." But he could afford to be magnanimous. "I say, though, that we should offer them terms . . ."

This speech by the Doge to his own people is reported by the Count de Villehardouin. Robert de Clari records his words to the assembled council of the Crusaders. "My Lords," he said, "you have betrayed our trust. From the moment that your ambassadors first made this proposition about the fleet, I have ensured that every aspect of business throughout my territories should be directed to the sole aim of furnishing your Crusade. This for a year and a half, even more. But my people have now lost a great deal—and that's the reason why they, and I too, are determined that you shall pay us the money you owe. And if you don't, then let me tell you that you shall not move a foot from the island until we have been paid. Quite apart from which, you will not find anyone who'll bring you anything to eat or drink."

It is hardly surprising that the barons and the others who heard these words retired from the Doge's presence, "distressed and very embarrassed".

In a speech to his own council, Doge Dandolo now made his intentions plain. No doubt there were some who were already saying that the Doge had not only saddled the Republic with a vast weight of bad debts but that they also had a large and potentially hostile army on their doorstep. Any sceptics as to the ability of the Doge to produce the finest possible solution—finest possible for his city-state, that is—were silenced before they could even murmur a complaint.

"The City of Zara has been taken from us by the King of Hungary," began the Doge. "It is, as we all know, one of the strongest cities in existence. With our own forces we have no hope of recapturing Zara. But what if we make use of the French? I suggest that we ask them to help us in this matter of Zara. If they do this, we will agree to postpone their payment of the 34,000 marks until they, and ourselves combined, have gained that amount of money by conquest."

There could be nothing but assent to such a brilliant suggestion. At one blow the Venetians would eliminate the threat that Zara represented to their Adriatic communications and trade. At one blow they would be free of the Crusaders, and there still remained a good chance that they would get full payment for the use of their fleet through any successes the Crusading armies might have over the Moslems.

The Doge can hardly have been surprised at the overwhelmingly favourable reception accorded to his speech. Knowing the situation that they were in, perhaps he was hardly less surprised when the barons and the inner council of knights reacted with an almost equal enthusiasm. He pointed out to them that it was already winter—hardly the time therefore to contemplate a long voyage across the Mediterranean. But if they came with him and the Venetians, and captured Zara, then they would be able to winter there in comfort. In the spring the fleet would reassemble and, with refreshed forces, the Crusade could proceed on its way, enriched by their share of the loot from Zara.

There were, of course, some dissentients, and some who murmured that they had not left their family estates to make war against a Christian city—even if it happened to be one with which the Venetians had some long-standing feud. They had come to fight against the heathen. They had come to redeem the Holy Places, so that Christian pilgrims could enjoy the right of visiting Jerusalem and making their devotions on that sacred earth where Christ had lived on his own pilgrimage through the world. "Not all of the army," writes Robert de Clari, "were happy about this decision [to attack Zara]—only the most important of the Crusaders." But decisions are taken by "the most important", and the barons realised only too clearly that they had no choice but accept the Doge's proposition.

Aware that there is nothing like a good gesture to convince the simple or the hesitant, Doge Dandolo now said that if the Crusaders were prepared to help him, he for his part would join with them and 'take the Cross'. The spectacle of this aged man, with "his sightless, but bright and clear eyes", kneeling weeping at the altar, as the Cross was sewn upon his cap, moved even the Venetians to tears. Thousands of the citizens hastened to join the Crusade themselves. The effect upon the French knights was electric, and even hardened foot soldiers were moved by the selfless abnegation of this old man (who had nevertheless ensured that if he went on the Crusade his son would act as his regent).*

The fact remains that, as a solution to their problems, the attack on Zara still horrified a great many of the Crusaders. Those who could manage to pay the extortionate sums demanded by Venetian boatmen had themselves ferried off Saint Nicholas island and quitted the Crusade. A contemporary historian described the feelings among the virtually imprisoned troops: "The proposal to attack Zara seemed cruel and iniquitous to our leaders, not only because it was a Christian city, but because it belonged to the King of Hungary. The King himself had taken the Cross and placed himself and his possessions (as is the custom) under the Pope's protection. Much time was lost, for the Venetians were constantly urging us to accept their proposition while we were equally concerned in refusing it . . . Our men thought it despicable, and contrary to moral law, that soldiers of the Cross of Christ should set out to slaughter and pillage fellow-Christians—for such was inevitably bound to happen in an assault on the city. They therefore refused to agree with the Venetian proposals." The obstinacy made no difference in the long run. Shortage of food and water, coupled with disease which had broken out among the troops crowded together on the small island, meant that in the end the army would be forced to comply with Dandolo's suggestion.

Remembering that the Pope had always suspected the Venetian connection with the Crusade, and that he had insisted on a papal legate accompanying the expedition, it is natural to inquire what this emissary of the Pope was doing during these months. Cardinal Peter of Capua, Innocent III's legate, did not arrive in Venice until the last week of July. As soon as he heard of the proposal made by the Doge to the leaders of the Crusade, he immediately registered his formal protest. He suggested that the army should embark immediately. That the Venetians had not been paid the full sum due to them was counterbalanced, in his opinion, by the fact that only about a third of the army that had originally been envisaged had arrived. Many of the prospective Crusaders, indeed, having heard the news from Venice as they made their way southward from Germany and France, had already halted and turned back.

But the Cardinal, although he might be the Pope's legate, counted for very little in Venetian eyes. He was ungraciously received, and told that he might accompany the Crusade if he wished—but only as a spiritual pastor and not as a Papal emissary. In the end, he too was forced to realise that the Venetians, or rather the Doge, had successfully trapped the Crusaders 'between the devil and the deep'. If they were to proceed at all to Egypt or Syria, they must pay the Venetian price—and that meant attacking Zara first of all. Possibly the Cardinal succumbed to that age-old fallacy, that the end justifies the means. Better, he may have thought, that the Crusade should set about its business against the infidel—even at the expense of a Christian city. The only alternative was the dissolution of the army, and with it the Pope's dream of a Crusade. The Cardinal had protested, but now he acquiesced.

In the first week of October 1202, 480 ships left Venice carrying the army of the Fourth Crusade for the attack on Zara. The fleet was a wonderful sight as it made its way through the Venetian lagoons bound for the high seas. Robert de Clari describes the magnificence of the galleys, and in particular that of the Doge, "painted vermilion, with a silk awning of vermilion spread above him, cymbals clashing, and four trumpeters sounding from the bows . . ." After touching at Trieste and Pola, the fleet arrived off Zara on November 11th.

It was clear that the people of Zara had been anticipating an attack by the Venetians, although they can hardly have envisaged that Doge Dandolo would manage to divert a crusading army for this purpose. They had forearmed themselves by securing a letter from the Pope which excommunicated any one who should attack them. This had as little effect upon the Doge as did the presence of Cardinal Peter. Despite protests from the Cistercian Abbot of Vaux (the only cleric apparently, who was unable to swallow his Christian principles), the city of Zara was attacked. It was captured on November 24th after five days' fighting.

The attack on Zara was a foretaste of what was to come, and of all the evil that was to follow in the wake of the Fourth Crusade. The city was sacked and looted, and the inhabitants were forced to take refuge in the hills. Zara's ancient churches were not spared by this army of Christians. Finally, in the course of their undisciplined looting, the Venetians and the Crusaders came to blows over the division of the spoils.

The whole episode was sordid and contemptible. It was contrary to every tenet, however slender, that had for centuries maintained the fabric of supposedly-Christian Europe. Innocent III on hearing the news was horrified and infuriated. He passed immediate sentence of excommunication upon all who had taken part—Venetians and Crusaders alike.

The effect of the Pope's action upon the ordinary Crusader can easily be imagined. He had left his home and family to take part in a 'sanctified' war against the heathen. Somehow or other he had been trapped into aiding the Venetians in a private act of warfare against a city belonging to the King of Hungary. Now he found that he was excommunicated, and he was still as far away as ever from the original object of his service. It was little wonder that relations between the ordinary soldiers and the Venetians became so bad as to end in open conflict. It was not only the loot that divided them, for the Crusaders felt ashamed of their action, and it took all the abilities of their leaders to patch up peace between the unwilling allies.

Throughout the winter that the army passed encamped in and around Zara, it was hardly surprising that there were many defections from the army. Some made their way north overland back to their homes, others who had the price of their passage embarked in visiting merchant ships. "Thus," Villehardouin wrote, "our forces dwindled from day to day."

From the very beginning of his account of the Fourth Crusade, Villehardouin placed most of the blame for the position in which the army found itself in Venice on the shoulders of those Crusaders who had made their own way to the Holy Land or Syria. It is indeed true that it was the failure of so many of the knights and soldiers to reach Venice which led to the inability of the Crusade to pay its way. At the same time, it is unlikely that Villehardouin was as ingenuous as he made out. He must have been aware that it would be impossible to calculate with any certainty just how many men would finally reach Venice. As one of the leaders of the Crusade, he needed to find every possible excuse for what occurred. It is hardly surprising, then, that one even finds him stigmatising as traitors the men who left the army after that gross violation of their Crusading oaths—the attack on Zara.

During the winter a deputation was sent to the Pope to beg him to lift his interdict from the army, and to restore them to the body of the Church. It was from these envoys that Innocent III heard the true story of what had happened. They explained how the Crusaders had been unable to pay the Venetians for the fleet, and how the Doge had proposed the attack on Zara as a solution to their difficulties. Their statement that they thought it better to keep the army together, and thus fulfil their ultimate purpose, rather than let it be disbanded before they had even left the island of Saint Nicholas, was no doubt true. Innocent III understood only too well what had happened— it was what he, with his knowledge of the Venetians, had always feared would befall the ingenuous Crusaders. But what was done could not be undone, and he could see no reason why the army should not proceed to Egypt in the spring of 1203. He agreed, therefore, to lift the penalty of excommunication from the Crusaders. As for the Doge and the Venetians, they were to remain excommunicated—a fact which does not seem to have troubled Enrico Dandolo unduly.

The loot taken in the sack on Zara was divided between the leaders of the army and the Venetians. Very little of it reached the men-at-arms and lesser knights, but even so the total does not seem to have amounted to very much. Certainly there was not enough to pay the Venetians the 34,000 marks that were outstanding. Meanwhile the men had to live and to buy provisions throughout the hard winter of the Adriatic. The result was that, when the spring came, they found that "they could neither go to Alexandria, nor Babylon, nor Syria, for they had already spent all their money both on their stay, and on the hire of the fleet . . .". The army's position was indeed as desperate as it had ever been. Now was the very moment for which the plotters had been waiting.

Doge Dandolo, we are told, "seeing that they were disturbed by their predicament", called a meeting and addressed them. "My Lords," he said, "there is in Greece a country that is rich, and well supplied with everything that you need. If we could only find a reasonable excuse to go there and take what we need to see us on our way, that would seem to me an ideal solution. In this way we could easily manage to get ourselves to the lands overseas." At this moment the Marquis of Montferrat rose to his feet and said: "My Lords, I have been staying during Christmas in Germany, at the court of the Emperor

[Philip of Swabia]. There I happened to meet a young man who is the brother of the Emperor's wife. This young man is the son of the Emperor Isaac of Constantinople, who was removed from the throne by the treason of one of his brothers. If we take this young man with us," he went on, "we could justifiably enter the territory of Constantinople, and there secure our stores and provisions, for he is indeed the legitimate Emperor."

Everything now had fallen into place. Like a massive and complex jigsaw puzzle, the schemes and ambitions of a number of individuals had dovetailed so that an overall pattern lay revealed—the diversion of the Fourth Crusade to Constantinople. Initially the Doge can have hoped for little more than the destruction of Zara, followed possibly by the dispersal of the Crusading army during the winter. But his dealings with Sultan al-Adil of Egypt were foremost in his mind, and he certainly had no intention of allowing the Crusaders to follow their initial plan and attack Egypt. There can be little doubt that he was privy to the plot of Philip of Swabia and Boniface of Montferrat.

The Crusaders, by falling into the Doge's trap, had placed themselves in a position where they were entirely dependent on the Venetians to transport them, and at Venice's terms. The Doge himself must have known of the presence of young Alexius at the German court since the summer of 1202. There can be no doubt that his speech to the Crusaders about the wealth and provisions to be obtained in Greece—so happily seconded by the speech of Montferrat providing in young Alexius the key to the problem—had been most carefully rehearsed. All that now remained was for Alexius to propose the solution to the Crusaders' difficulties. He accordingly stated that, if they would place him upon the throne of the Byzantine Empire, he would pay them 200,000 marks. This would enable them to pay their debt to Venice, and would provide them with more than enough capital to prosecute their campaign. At the same time, Alexius guaranteed them an army of 10,000 men. This would more than make good the deficiencies caused by those who had failed to join them, or by those who had subsequently deserted.

In the desperate position in which they found themselves there could be no doubt what the response of many would be. There were still some dissentients, but these were overruled. The Crusade was diverted yet again. On May 4th, the fleet and the Crusading army, having left Zara, put into the harbour of Corfu. A few days later two galleys joined them, bringing down the principal actors in the drama: Dandolo, Doge of Venice, Boniface, Marquis of Montferrat, and Alexius, pretender to the throne of Byzantium. Despite the fact that a considerable number of the more important barons and knights, among them Simon de Montfort, had already left the army, refusing to betray their Crusading oaths any further ('traitors,' according to the Count de Villehardouin), it was still an immense fleet which anchored in Corfu roads.

This was the last moment when any effective protest could have been made against the diversion of the Crusade. It was hardly surprising that even at this late hour there were a number of barons and knights who suddenly realised the trap into which they had fallen. The 'malcontents', as Villehardouin calls them, divided themselves from the rest of the army, took with them a considerable number of soldiers who also had no wish to go to Constantinople, and set up a separate camp and parliament. Realising that with their small numbers they would be unable to attack Egypt, they decided to make their way to Syria, where they knew that a number of the earlier defectors from the Crusade had already arrived.

There was consternation among the leaders at this further division of the army. They debated how best to convince them that the only solution for all their problems was to proceed to Constantinople. When all other devices fail, it often pays to fall back upon the simplest and most emotional of tricks to secure one's object—such was the Doge's experience.

Together with Boniface and the other leaders of the Crusade, he went on foot to the camp of the mutineers and fell at their feet. He begged them with tears not to break up so great and noble an army. "Do not leave us!" he and his companions cried, all weeping bitterly. "We will not rise from the ground until you tell us that you will not leave us!"

The thought of Enrico Dandolo and the Marquis of Montferrat, accompanied by Alexius, kneeling in that green glade in Corfu with the tears coursing down their cheeks is not without its humour. Even seven centuries later one seems to see those crocodile tears, and witness the consternation spread like panic over the simple faces of their audience.

Like so many who are strong in the arm, the Crusaders were not so well-endowed in the head. They could not bear to see these great and noble men kneeling in the grass at their feet. They agreed not to break up the army, to proceed with their leaders, and to secure from the Byzantines such food and provisions as might be needed. They made only one stipulation: that after Michaelmas Day (September 29th) they must be provided with ships and provisions to go on their way to Syria. This was willingly agreed to. By September, Dandolo and Boniface felt sure that their objective would have been attained —and even if it had not, they would by then be at Constantinople. The opposition (if there was any by that time) would be dependent on Venetian ships to get them south. There could be no chance of part of the army leaving at such a juncture, and fighting its way to Syria through a hostile Asia Minor dominated by the Turks.

Such was the dismal and bitter story that lay behind the diversion of the Fourth Crusade to Constantinople. Few episodes in history reveal more clearly the cynicism of the higher command or the stupidity of the masses. As it had begun, so it would continue. Those who realised that they had been tricked, would soon enough find some justification for their acts. Those who had tricked them were already conjuring up the explanations which they would ultimately be forced to make.

5

THE FLEET ENTERS THE GOLDEN HORN

On the morning of July 5th, 1203, the galleys of the Venetians preceded the main body of the fleet across the narrow passage from Chrysopolis on the Asiatic coast to the shore below the suburb of Galata, on the northern side of the Golden Horn. This stretch of coastline was neither walled, nor defended, and Galata, a Jewish and international settlement, was not unfriendly to a force of French, Venetians and other fellow-Catholics. The only real defence-point of the city that lay north of the Horn itself was a large tower, known as the castle of Galata.

Unmolested during its crossing of the Bosphorus, the fleet came safely to anchor within a few cables of the shore. The transports and landing-craft touched down on the beach itself, near the modern suburb of Tophane. South of here, along the banks of the Golden Horn, lay the Jewish quarter of the city. Unbelievable though it seemed that an invading fleet should be able to cross the Bosphorus unopposed, it could hardly be expected that—even in the days of the Emperor Alexius—the troops would be permitted to land without some show of resistance.

The Crusaders themselves were prepared for a fierce opposition and had boarded the ships, armed and ready. Their helmets were laced, their war-horses were saddled and caparisoned. In that period, the 'destriers', or war-horses of the knights, were covered with a lengthy trapping of taffeta, blazoned with the arms of the knight and reaching almost to the horse's hooves. The knights themselves wore suits of chain-mail, a type of defensive armour which had been evolved during the Crusades, and which derived from the interlaced chain-mail that the early Crusaders had found in use among their Moslem foes. Articulated pieces of plate-mail covered their knees, while the rest of their legs were protected with chain-mail which laced at the back. The arms and upper part of the body were covered by a jacket of mail, also lacing at the back, and reaching half-way down the thighs. Incorporated in this jacket was a mailed cap which laced up either at the back, or on the left side of the head. Over the mail coat it was customary to wear a surcoat or jupon—a loose-flowing linen garment, usually white to deflect the heat of the sun. On it was displayed the owner's blazon, or often in the case of Crusaders simply embroidered with the Cross. The object of the surcoat was to distinguish one individual from another in the heat of battle.

Suspended from a baldric (a sword-belt hung from one shoulder to the opposite hip) was the sheath and sword. The latter was of the straight-edged European type (as opposed to the curved scimitar of the East) and was usually sharpened on both sides of its length—double-edged—although some single-edged swords were still in use. This was basically a cutting sword, although the point could be used for thrusting, but a great many of the swords of this period were too heavy to be used in this manner. Some of them were of the two-handed type, requiring considerable physical strength to lift, and leaving the swordsman totally unprotected, except for his armour, once they were raised in the air. From the height of a horse, however, such heavy swords had their advantages, particularly when used against other knights on horseback, or against foot soldiers.

Beneath their chain-mail the Crusaders wore a padded garment, both to keep their skins from contact with the mail itself (which would be hot under an eastern sun) and to check the shock when they were struck by an opponent. "It is one of the mysteries in the history of armour," wrote C. J. Ffoulkes, "how the Crusaders can have fought under the scorching sun of the East in thick quilted garments covered with excessively heavy chain-mail, for this equipment was so cumbersome to take on and off that it must have been worn frequently day and night, and the very nature of the fabric made it almost impossible to move the sword arm with more than a wide swinging cut . . ." *

Hot indeed it was, and there are several accounts of armoured men dropping dead from heart-attack or heat-exhaustion. Another drawback to chain-mail was that, in the action of raising a sword to cut at an opponent, the mail automatically collected into folds at the elbow joint. At the same time some effort was needed to raise the arm, because of the weight of the mail jerkin as it lifted from the waist upwards. Nevertheless, it had been found from the experience of several centuries that an armoured man possessed considerable advantage over an unarmoured opponent. One thing is certain, there was a distinct benefit to morale in belonging to an armoured body of troops, and the psychological effect of the sight of these steel-clad men glistening in the sun on their caparisoned horses could have a terrifying effect upon an unarmoured enemy. Apart from anything else, the armoured knight had his head protected, not only by his mail head-piece but usually by a helmet made of steel plate.

Since the eleventh century the Normans had made use of an efficient conical headpiece, with a nose-guard to protect the face against sword-cuts, while the design of the helmet was such that it presented a glancing surface to almost all angles of attack. At the time of the Fourth Crusade, however, the 'barrel helm' was fashionable. This was a headpiece which, except that it was comparatively easy to make, seems to have had little to recommend it. Completely enclosing the head, the barrel helm had a flat top (thus presenting the worst kind of surface to a blow). It was supported on the wearer's head by a padded cap —with the result that, if the helm was struck a smart blow on the side, it was liable to swivel round. Once this had happened the wearer was unable to see through the eye-slits and was completely defenceless. But even the barrel helm was better than having no head armour at all. The Crusaders were not necessarily better soldiers than the Byzantine troops with whom they were soon to come in conflict—indeed, at the peak of its excellence, the Byzantine army had been the best in the world.

The Crusaders, however, had a higher morale and they had the best of modern European armour. Their opponents were only lightly armoured. Mobility had always been the secret of the success of the Byzantine infantry, while the weight behind their attacks had been provided by an armoured cavalry.

On the morning of July 5th, as the Crusaders neared the shore at Galata, "it was bright after the sun had risen, and the Emperor Alexius, with his army in great force drawn up in array, awaited them on the shore. The trumpets sounded. Each transport was attached to a galley by a tow-rope (to make the passage quicker). No one asked who should go first, for each made for the shore at its best possible speed. The knights leaped down from the transports, fully armed, with their helmets laced and their lances in hand. As soon as each vessel touched the ground, the well-trained sergeants, archers, and crossbowmen followed the knights . . ."

All Constantinople watched. "When the people of the city saw the great fleet and army, and heard the sound of the drums and trumpets, making a tremendous noise, all of them without exception armed themselves and stood on the roofs of their houses. It must have seemed to them as if the sea and the earth were shaking, and as if all the water was covered with ships. Meanwhile the emperor had come down with his armed forces to the shore to defend it . . ."

Now indeed was the moment when, if the Byzantines were to prevent the occupation of the northern shore of the Golden Horn, they must throw the enemy back into the sea. But the violence of the Crusaders' landing appalled them. The speed with which the horses and men disembarked, and the spectacle of hundreds of ships discharging their troops with disciplined precision was too much for their debilitated morale. At the first shock of lances the Byzantines broke and fled. The field was left to the Crusaders, who were able to disembark the main body of the army at their leisure. These latter-day Byzantines had fallen into such a state of cowardice and indiscipline that they offered practically no resistance to the arrival of a hostile army at the gates of their city. Two centuries before, their ancestors under the great Emperor Basil the Bulgar-Slayer had been of different fibre. They had held all Asia Minor as far east as the Tigris; Southern Italy, most of Sicily, and North Africa as far west as Tripoli had been theirs, together with Egypt and all the Levant. But in the past hundred years a succession of weak emperors, corrupt administration, the eternal blood-drain caused by the Turkish onslaughts, and the decline of shipping and trade had sapped Byzantine strength and morale. As for the present Emperor, his people had as little faith in him as in his blinded predecessor. No doubt there were many among them who felt that, rather than oppose this large and disciplined army, they would do better to withdraw within the walls of their impregnable city. So many times had barbarians from all points of the compass come against it, and so many times had the aggressors withdrawn, discouraged and defeated. Surely, they may have felt, the same would happen now with these rough Franks, Venetian pirates and Norman bandits.

"The sailors now started to open the sally-ports of the trans-ports and let down the gangplanks for the horses. The knights mounted swiftly, while all the divisions started to draw up in their appointed order . . ." Despite all the dissensions in Venice, despite the bitter winter in Zara, and despite the recent differences in Corfu, the army was still a disciplined and efficient force. It is interesting evidence of the profession of men-at-arms at this period that a mixed army from several countries, led by barons and knights from France, Belgium, Germany and Italy, could still—even after a sea-passage—emerge as an organised unit ready for immediate battle. "And now Count Baldwin of Flanders, who commanded the vanguard, rode forward, followed by the other divisions in battle array, until they reached the place where the Emperor Alexius had been encamped." The flight of the Greeks had been so precipitous that they had not even stopped to dismantle the Emperor's pavilion, nor those of his senior officers. Overjoyed at the success of their landing, the Crusaders now found themselves in possession of easy loot— and all within an hour of the campaign beginning.

The slower ships in the fleet now followed the invasion forces. In the centre of the Bosphorus they felt the tug of the current running down from the Black Sea to the Sea of Marmora. Then, as they neared the shore, they met the gentle counter-current flowing northwards. Dropping anchor, the large merchantmen and store-ships rode easily with their bows to the south. Sailors began ferrying ashore the wooden parts of siege-engines and catapults, and transferring stores and provisions from the large ships to the base camp. Meanwhile, the army was digging in against any surprise attack by the Byzantine cavalry.

The leaders had decided to encamp on the southern tip of land, facing across the Golden Horn towards the city. This position was near the tower or castle of Galata, that strong defence-point on which depended the security of the inner harbour of the Horn. The Doge, Baldwin of Flanders and the other barons were well aware that the success or failure of the expedition lay upon their ability to capture this tower. If they could take it, the whole of the northern shores facing Constantinople would be in their hands. Even more important was the fact that, once the tower was theirs, the Venetian fleet could sweep into the Horn, capture the merchant shipping lying there at anchor, and secure the army access to the walls of the city itself.

The tower of Galata was designed not only as a fortress to guard the northern entrance to the Horn but as the terminal point for the great chain upon which the safety of the harbour depended. Stretched between the tower and the city walls there ran an immense chain, operated by a windlass. When the chain was hauled up bar-taut, it hung a few feet above the surface of the sea—thus preventing any ship from entering the harbour. When shipping wished to enter, the chain was lowered away until vessels could pass over it without obstruction. The huge iron links, each the length of a forearm, had been made by the skilled ironworkers of the city. Technical skill indeed was needed to construct a chain with sufficient tensile strength to reach over 1,500 feet—the width of the harbour at this point—as well as to submit to the stresses and strains of being constantly raised and lowered.

The tower itself was "strong, easy to defend", according to de Clari, "and very well garrisoned". Intended as one of the strong-points of the city's defences, it should indeed have been easy enough to hold—although it had never been designed with the idea in mind that it would have to resist a prolonged siege by an enemy whose fleet commanded the Bosphorus. The defences of the tower of Galata had been thought of as providing no more than a check-point, while the Byzantine fleet destroyed the fleet of the attacker. But in the reign of the Emperor Alexius the fleet was to all intents and purposes non-existent. The tower, therefore, stood on its own. No ships had opposed the Crusaders' landing, and the tower must now submit to the full weight of a land-attack by a large army which could bring up siege engines and catapults against it.*

Even at this moment of national decadence, when the Byzantines had no regard for their emperor, and when they were passing through one of those phases of human existence when the battle for survival seems hardly worthwhile, they were not so lost to a sense of values as to disregard the tower of Galata. They knew as well as the Venetians that the safety of the harbour depended upon it and therefore, probably, of Constantinople itself. According to the Greek historian Nicetas it was the Emperor's brother-in-law, Theodore Lascaris, who proposed aggressive action against the invaders of the ancient kingdom.*

During the first night that the Crusaders were encamped against the city near the Galata tower, the Greeks prepared to make a desperate effort to prevent its capture. They manned a number of small boats and sent word across to the garrison in the tower that they would join them in an attack on the Crusaders early the following morning. It was the usual cry of "Too little, and too late!" Once the enemy had been allowed to establish a safe beach-head on the foreshore, there was little or no chance of dislodging them without making a major assault on their position. A half-hearted attempt was doomed to failure.

Early next morning, July 6th, the Greek troops who had been ferried across from the city joined up with the garrison from the tower of Galata, and attacked the army of the Fourth Crusade. It was an example of the worst kind of tactical error. There was little or no element of surprise about it for very naturally, "the army had kept a vigilant watch all night". To have any chance of success it should have been prosecuted with the utmost vigour, and with a great weight of arms. As it was, a comparatively small detachment of the Greek army, aided by some of the defenders of the tower, attempted to rout a vigilant army of Crusaders, numbering about 20,000 men.

The result was a foregone conclusion. The Crusaders rallied to the defence and, within a matter of minutes, the attackers were fleeing for their lives. "The alarm was given throughout the camp, and the men rallied round from all sides. They charged the Greeks so fiercely that not only were many of them killed, but many were over-run and taken prisoner . . ." It was at a time like this that the mounted knights proved their worth, just as much as in formal cavalry charges. An armed man on horseback, pursuing fleeing infantrymen, had every advantage —speed, security and above all self-confidence. An armoured, mounted man felt himself doubly secure, for he had his armoured advantage over his opponent, while at the same time his horse gave him a fleetness and mobility that no infantryman —except in hill country—could ever match.

Now, as they turned in flight, the Byzantines (whose own cavalry had once dominated the battle-fields of Asia Minor and eastern Europe), heard behind them the war-cries of mounted men—and the sound of the war-horse, which "goeth on to meet the armed men. He mocketh at fear, and is not affrighted; neither turneth he his back from the sword. The quiver rattleth against him, the glittering spear and the shield. He swalloweth the ground with fierceness and rage; neither believeth he that it is the sound of the trumpet. He saith among the trumpets, Ha, ha; and he smelleth the battle afar off, the thunder of the captains, and the shouting."

The Greeks had gravely miscalculated their opponents and now, in their haste to escape, they committed the gravest error of all. They forgot, or were unable, to shut the gate of the tower behind them. As the soldiers who had been ferried over from Constantinople rushed to regain their transports, "many of them being drowned in the process", the troops from the tower were overtaken by the Crusaders. Heavy fighting took place around the entrance, but it was too late by now to check the onward rush of the Crusaders. They stormed Galata tower, and killed or captured all the Byzantine defenders. It was only a matter of minutes for the Venetians—those men trained to the ways of the sea and its attendant crafts like anchors and cables—to dismantle the windlass and unshackle the great cable. With a rattling sigh, like the last gasp of a dying man, the great iron chain slid into the sea and sagged to the bottom of the Golden Horn. The way was now open for the ships of Venice.

There was no resistance from the few vessels of the Byzantine navy moored in the harbour. The fleet which had once patrolled the Mediterranean from the strait of Gibraltar to the island of Cyprus and the shores of the Levant was reduced to a few out-of-commision, old or decrepit galleys. Even while the tide of battle was flowing around Galata tower, the galleys of Venice were backing and filling off the Horn, their iron beaks poised over the chain that forbade them entrance. When the cheers from ashore told them the outcome of the battle, they waited to see the barrier before them slip out of sight. The moment that the barnacled-bespattered links dropped into the water, the galley captains gave the order. The slaves bent over the looms of the oars and, with a soft sigh of bow-waves, the spearhead of the Venetian fleet sped into the tranquil harbour—the blue waters of the Golden Horn that had helped to make Constantinople the richest city in Christendom. "And so they took the galleys of the Greeks and the other vessels that were in the harbour." By the morning of the following day the whole of the Venetian fleet—transports, galleys, merchantmen and store-ships—was safely at anchor inside the Golden Horn.

From the long line of the northern walls—weakest point in the circuit of Constantinople—the inheritors of the Byzantine Empire watched the capture of Galata tower, and the collapse of the great chain. Never before had an enemy of Constantinople penetrated into the Horn itself. The city had not been designed to withstand the attack of a maritime power which could control these waters. It had always been understood that the Byzantine fleet would prevent any landings in the Galata area, let alone a breakthrough beyond the chain barrier. The result was that the city walls fronting the Horn were comparatively weak. Unlike the great landward walls to the west, designed in their triple row to withstand any attack from Bulgar, Slav, Turk or Russian—unlike the seaward walls designed to dominate any seaborne landings—the northern walls of the city were more of a secondary defence.

Entrenched behind their centuries of power and prowess, the citizens of Constantinople had forgotten that time erodes, and that all things change. They were Greeks—even though, as inheritors of the Roman Empire, they called themselves 'Romans'. But perhaps they had never known the words of a Greek philosopher who had been dead many centuries before ever the religion of Christ came out of the land of Palestine: "Everything flows." That had been the philosophical principle of Heraclitus, the 'Dark Philosopher' as he was called on account of his lonely life, the profundity of his philosophy, and his contempt for humanity. "In nature the sole actuality is change." This was the bitter truth that the Greeks of the Christian Faith would soon be forced to learn.

6

THE FIRST ASSAULT

AFTER the capture of the tower and the occupation of the harbour by their fleet, it would have been natural for the barons to send envoys to the Emperor, asking him if he were now prepared to treat with them. The last communication that had taken place between the Doge, the barons and the Emperor Alexius III had been Conon de Béthune's speech to the Lombard Nicholas Roux. The gist of this had been that the Crusaders intended to place young Alexius on the throne, and that they would endeavour to secure the present emperor's safety and subsequent prosperity, if he would abdicate. Naturally enough Alexius III had ignored their message. But if the Crusaders had had any wish to avoid a siege, their recent victory offered a good opportunity to see whether their terms were at all acceptable. Nothing was done. None of the historians of these events mentions any further attempts at negotiations.

The Venetian soldiers and sailors, and the young knights and Crusaders, were no doubt so elated at the success of their landing and of their first encounter with the enemy that they never stopped to wonder what was their objective. They had been seized by the sharp joy of warfare and by an awareness that they had the upper hand. There was no reason, then, for them to call a halt or consider why the Byzantine was an enemy at all. The prospect of easy loot lured them on. Doge Dandolo, Boniface of Montferrat and the other accomplices in the plot had no longer any reason to fear that their army would desert or fail them.

If Alexius had been anything more than a tool, now surely would have been the moment for him to insist that a delegation be sent to his uncle offering him terms. The Emperor had now seen the superior spirit of this Crusading army and must have realised how little he could count on his own troops. He might well have agreed to abdicate. Alexius could then have entered Constantinople in triumph, backed by Crusading arms, delivered his father from the imperial dungeons, and taken over the throne. It can have been no wish of his that the city should be damaged in a siege, let alone sacked and looted. It was clearly in his interests to inherit an intact property. If he did nothing, it was because he could do nothing. Against the worldly wisdom and experience of advisers like the Doge, what had youthful inexperience to offer? As a Greek of the Orthodox Faith, he was dependent upon these Roman Christians for his acquisition of the scarlet buskins, the imperial mantle and the golden crown of the most ancient throne in Europe. It was only by their swords, courage and cunning that he had any chance of calling himself "Heir of the universal Roman Empire and Viceregent of God Himself".

There could be no doubt in the minds of the leaders as to what their next move should be. After so swift and sudden a success, no military man could fail to see that every advantage must be taken of the situation. While the Emperor Alexius, his court, his generals, his troops and people, were still overcome by the shock of these early reverses, the Crusaders should spring to the attack. Deliberation would be fatal, and to strike again swiftly was the obvious key to victory. The only question about which there could be any doubt was how best to achieve this. The Venetians, as was natural to a sea-power, were the first to realise the importance of their supremacy inside the Golden Horn. They argued for an immediate seaborne attack on the northern walls of the city. The French and the other Crusaders protested, for their part, that they were not sailors, and that they would be wasting their special abilities by coming as marine troops aboard the galleys. It was clear that the best solution was "for the French to besiege the city by land, while the Venetians attacked by sea". Doge Dandolo agreed to the apparent wisdom of this plan, and ordered the Venetians to start preparing siege machinery.

The next four days were spent by the army and navy in making ready for the assault on Constantinople. The sailors were busy stitching together hides to make tents over the fore-parts of their vessels—so that the anticipated deluge of Greek fire from the walls of the city would fall upon well-wetted hides, instead of on sun-dried wooden decks. At the same time, "The Doge of Venice gave orders for some extraordinary and ingenious devices to be made . . ."

These were long gangways made out of the lateen sail-yards of the galleys, many of which were about 180 feet long. Two of these lateen yards were used as the side-supporters to construct a bridge, while planks of wood were nailed or lashed between them to form the bridge-surface itself. Heavy awnings of sail-cloth were erected on poles above these bridges to give pro-tection to the troops who would use them.

These landing bridges were placed aboard the large merchant ships and were suspended, rather like movable gangplanks, from their masts by means of rope tackles. They were further secured by other cables to the ships' sides and bulwarks, and were so designed that they projected from the bows of the ships about 120 feet, raised slightly at an angle so that the ends of the bridges would be level with the top of the city walls. The con-struction of these bridges in so short a time was a remarkable feat of engineering. But this was not the first time that the Venetians had assaulted walled cities from the sea, and the ease and speed with which they were assembled suggests that plans for their use had been evolved long before the arrival of the ships at Constantinople. "They were so well constructed and so screened," according to de Clari, "that the soldiers who had to use them were never troubled by arrows or missiles from above . . . and they were so wide that three armoured knights could march up them abreast."

Mangonels (rock-hurling catapults) were assembled in the bows of other transports, while catapults and wooden towers for attacking the walls were dragged round to the head of the harbour for use by the army. The Venetians would attack the walls of the city facing the Horn, while the Crusaders would concentrate the weight of their thrust against the palace of

Blachernae. Near where the land walls met the Golden Horn, at the far end of this great harbour and at the north-west corner of the city, stood the immense complex of buildings called Blachernae, Palace of the Emperors.

Blachernae had originally been a suburb of Constantinople, standing outside the walls of the city. But from the twelfth century onward, the emperors had tended to move their residence here, preferring the situation to the Sacred Palace in the city near Santa Sophia. Blachernae was free from the noise and smoke of the capital, and gave the emperors and their court easy access to the hunting-grounds in the nearby country. Rising tier upon tier up the slopes of a small hill, the palace was a self-contained city—resembling in this the Kremlin of the Muscovite Tsars (itself of Byzantine derivation)—for it was a palace, a fortress, a religious centre and a seat of industry all in one. Goldsmiths and silk-weavers, craftsmen in wood and ivory, illuminators of manuscripts and mosaic-workers formed a steady procession through its gates. Although the main centre of their activities was in the Sacred Palace, the growth of Blachernae had focused a new interest on this far corner of Constantinople, where the small river of Barmyssa flowed out into the Golden Horn. From the top of the hill there was a wonderful view over the harbour, and over the city. The Crusader Odon de Deuil remarked of it that "it gives its inhabitants a threefold pleasure, for it looks over sea, meadow and city".

In the seventh century a wall had been built around Blachernae, and fifty years before this present attack the Emperor Manuel I had further strengthened the whole quarter. At the head of the Horn, just where the river flowed into the sea, a stone bridge led across from the northern side to Blachernae. It was at this point that the main weight of the attack was to fall—the Venetians sweeping in by sea against the walls, while the army fell on the Blachernae area by land. All the ships and troops were accordingly moved up to this far corner of the Horn, so that their blow could be coordinated. As soon as they saw the intention of the invaders, the Byzantines broke down the bridge over the Barmyssa, closed the gate of Blachernae and manned their defences. On July 11th, five days after their capture of Galata tower, the Crusading army marched up in formal array and prepared to lay siege to Blachernae.

The first necessity was to repair the bridge so that the mounted knights might cross without difficulty, and the siege-engines be brought up to the walls. This was no more than a day and a night's work. Early on the following morning the troops crossed the river and drew up within range of the city. During their crossing they had neither been attacked nor even harrassed by the Byzantines. *Quem Deus vult perdere, dementat prius*—it was almost incredible that the opportunity of attacking an enemy at such a moment should have been neglected. Perhaps the Greeks were confident in the strength of their city walls and felt that no further effort was necessary. Perhaps they relied upon divine sources for their protection. In the church of St. Peter and St. Mark at Blachernae there was the incorruptible, sweet-smelling robe of Our Lady (removed from Capernaum in Palestine in the fifth century), together with Her wonder-working icon. Every Friday, as the erudite Princess Anna Comnena has described in her memoirs of the court, the veil in front of this icon parted miraculously, to reveal the presence of the Mother of God to the assembled faithful.

The army set up camp within catapult range of the Blachernae walls, choosing as their base a fortified abbey on a slight mound, called 'The Castle of Bohemond' after a Crusader who had earlier passed this way. From this position, where they settled down to prepare for the siege and to repel any attacks that the defenders might make, the troops had a magnificent view of the awe-inspiring stretch of the city walls as they ran southward, to fade away into the folds of land several miles away. "It was a sight to fill the heart both with exultation and apprehension. So great was the extent of the land-walls that the most our army could manage was to besiege but one of all the many gates . . ."

The Venetians and the Crusaders had chosen well in deciding to launch their attack upon this corner of the city. Blachernae was undoubtedly the weak point in the defences. It had never been fortified to the same extent as Constantinople proper, for it had never been expected that an enemy would be able to control the waters of the Horn. But the main land-walls, at which the Crusaders gazed in simple wonder, had been designed to repel the attacks of armies many times the size of theirs. The Theodosian wall, as it was called, ran from Blachernae in a huge unbroken line, all the way south to the sea of Marmora. Its construction was the triumph of Anthemius, Regent and Prefect during the reign of Theodosius II in the fifth century.

Although restored over the centuries, and improved in a few minor details, this main shield of the city was little changed from its initial conception. The main, or inner, wall was fifteen feet thick, and about forty feet high. From it projected no less than ninety-six battlemented towers, strong points which could provide a covering fire between one and another. The thickness of the main wall was more than sufficient to resist the siege engines of the thirteenth century, but it was not only upon this that the city relied. The defence of Constantinople was a triple one. Beyond the inner wall there ran a *peribolos*, or terrace, some forty feet in width, and beyond this rose yet another wall only slightly less formidable than the inner. This was about twenty-five feet high and also had a regular series of towers protecting it (spaced about one hundred yards apart). Beyond this again there was a further stretch of open ground, called the *Para-teichion*, and then a further outer breastwork wall, suitable for sheltering archers and crossbowmen. Beyond this again there lay an immense ditch, some fifty feet wide. Normally kept dry, the ditch could be flooded as and where required by a complicated system of dams. Hidden deep beneath the ditch and the three sequences of walls, there flowed the city's water supply. It was carried in seven-inch-diameter pipes to feed the reservoirs, and the private and municipal buildings in the city itself. Constantinople's security against siege was further reinforced by immense underground reservoirs within the city.

Protected by the splendour of these walls, the Byzantines had maintained their city and civilisation for eight centuries. Constructed of limestone blocks, interspaced with courses of brick, they were among the most astounding of Byzantine achievements. Even the walls of Rhodes and Malta, built centuries later by the Knights of St. John, could hardly compare with the strength and the complexity of these defences. Yet it was possibly because of a sense of security induced by these walls—a 'Maginot mentality'—that the citizens of Constantinople had grown complacent. Walls are made by men, and in the final analysis it is only upon the strength and morale of the men who defend them that true security may be found. The walls of Constantinople required for their defence a large and well-disciplined army. This was something that they had lacked for many years.

Once it was clear that the Crusaders seriously intended to lay siege to the city, the Byzantines began to take action. Some of the aggressive spirit that they now began to show may be traced to the same Theodore Lascaris, who had promoted the earlier attack on the Crusaders. "There was not an hour either of the day or night when one of our divisions did not have to stand guard opposite Blachernae to preserve the siege-engines and ward off sorties made by the defenders. At least six or seven times a day the army had to be called to the defence. It was impossible to forage for provisions more than four bowshots from our camp. Hardly any food was left except flour and a little salted-down meat—and no fresh meat at all except when a horse was killed."

The Crusaders had been short of provisions ever since leaving Corfu. Indeed, it was in order to victual the army that they had (technically at least) first ventured in Byzantine territory. Confronted with the ominous vista of the landward walls of the city, there were many who must have felt that they had undertaken more than they could perform. There was no sign of the Byzantines being willing to treat with them, and no sign that they wished to have 'this Alexius' made their emperor. Doge Dandolo was well aware that the only solution to their difficulties lay in a successful seaborne attack on the city. He was far too old and experienced in warfare to believe that the Crusaders could storm the Theodosian walls of Constantinople.

By July 17th the Doge was ready. His ships were equipped with their siege-engines and their drawbridges. He knew that it was upon the success or failure of his own Venetians that the whole campaign depended, and he had not been willing to hasten the matters unduly until his galley-masters had assured him that they were fully prepared. The Crusaders, meanwhile, had established themselves in a good base-camp, well protected by stakes and palisade from Byzantine cavalry attacks. The shortage of food in the army produced its automatic deadline. The attacks of the Byzantines grew increasingly desperate as they realised that the real threat against their defences was yet to come.

Villehardouin tells how "Hardly a day passed without a skirmish—so many that I cannot remember them all . . ." For ten days the army had endured these attacks, growing ever shorter of food, and ever more concerned about its position. It is evidence of the dogged determination of men who joined Crusading armies that they did not despair in front of those seemingly impregnable walls. No fanatical impulse of faith had driven them to their encamped position beneath Blachernae. No religious impulse made them feel that they were preparing to fight and die in the spirit of Jesus Christ against an infidel horde. The hair-splitting finesses of dogma that may have led their priests to believe that Greek Christians were heretics were quite beyond the simple soldier. Nothing held this army together but the prospect of loot—and the fact that from this remote corner of Europe there could be no turning back. The Doge of Venice and his fellow-conspirators had shown a shrewd insight into the nature of the fighting man.

On Thursday morning, July 17th, 1203, the great attack took place. "The Venetians were already on their way across the Golden Horn, their scaling ladders prepared for the assault, and the army was drawn up for battle. Three divisions were left on guard at the camp, while the remaining four marched to attack the city." The engagement began with an assault on a barbican close to the sea. This was most probably one of the towers guarding the seaward gate of Blachernae. It was good tactics to concentrate on this point, since the Venetian galleys were able to bring their attack to bear on the adjacent walls. Catapults launched their bolts from both ships and land at the threatened position. Meanwhile French troops ran up two ladders against the barbican and prepared to scale it.

But the barbican defences, as Nicetas tells us, were manned by the Emperor's crack troops, "the Pisans and the Warings". Villehardouin mentions only the latter, calling them "Englishmen and Danes", and gives them great credit for the gallantry of their defence. Although two knights and two sergeants, followed by fifteen men-at-arms, managed to scale the barbican they were swiftly repelled, "in a hand-to-hand battle of swords against battle-axes." This is a further confirmation that it was indeed the Waring guard which held this threatened corner of the city. It was only the Warings among Byzantium's international army who carried the battle-axe.

The Warings' counter-attack routed the French, who were driven off the barbican, two of their men being taken prisoner. " . . . They were taken before the Emperor Alexius who was delighted at this proof of his men's prowess. Such was the outcome of the attack by land, and the barons were greatly disheartened, for many of the French had been wounded or left with broken limbs." But if the efforts of the army were in vain, the ships of Venice under the leadership of the Doge were having a remarkable success. Extended in a long line they came on slowly to the sweep of their great oars, while the mangonels on their foredecks kept up a steady fire on the walls. Meanwhile the bowmen and crossbowmen stood ready and, as soon as they were within range, released their showers of iron quarrels and arrows at the defenders. As the ladders in the bows of the assault-craft neared the walls, the men gathered in the tunnel-like bridges were able to fire directly at their opponents. Some even came so close to the walls that the men in the front rank were exchanging sword-thrusts with the defenders. "The noise was so great that the sea and the land seemed to shake . . ."

Curiously enough, no mention is made of the use of Greek Fire, that sovereign remedy upon which the fate of the city had so often depended. Possibly this was because, on the walls facing the Golden Horn, there were few outlets for Greek Fire such as existed on the seaward walls of the Marmora. The Doge's wisdom in having the assault bridges and fore-parts of the ships covered with hides may possibly have prevented any serious damage arising from its use. But there can be no doubt that, even if there were no major flame-throwers incorporated in this part of the city walls, there will have been hand-held trumps in use among the defenders.

The trump was a hollow tube of metal or wood, through which a hand-bellows pumped a combustible mixture of resin and sulphur. Linseed oil was among the other ingredients used to produce the inflammable liquid. When fire was applied to the mouth of the trump, "it continues a long time snorting and belching vivid, furious flames that shoot out for several yards". A Russian fleet which had once attacked the Marmora walls had been routed by flame-throwers. On a previous occasion when a Crusading army had been looting Byzantine islands on their way to the Holy Land, the Pisan fleet that carried them had been put to flight by the Byzantine admiral, who had ordered his ships to be equipped with flame-throwers. "On the prow of each ship he had a head of a lion or other land animal fixed, made in brass or iron with the mouth open, and gilded over so that the mere aspect was terrifying. And the fire which was to be directed against the enemy through tubes he made to pass through the mouths of the beasts, so that it seemed as if the lions and other monsters were vomiting fire . . ." At the siege of Durazzo in 1107, when the Byzantines had been in conflict with the Normans, they had run a counter-mine against a tunnel that the Normans were digging beneath the city. Bursting in on the Norman sappers, they had routed them by turning flame-throwers upon them.

But these successes lay in the past. There were no Byzantine ships now to challenge the Venetians upon the waters of the Horn, while the omission of any mention of Greek fire during this action suggests that it was not used, or ineffective. But even though the Venetians managed to get their ships right up to the walls, they were unwilling to beach them on the strip of fore-shore beneath the battlements. It was at this moment that the Doge showed that he still retained the spirit which had made him a great leader. "Old and blind though he was, he stood in the prow of his galley, while above him waved the banner of St. Mark. He cried out to his men to drive on for the shore unless they wished to incur his utmost displeasure. Then, as the galley's bows grounded, he and they leapt out and planted the banner of St. Mark on the shore. As soon as the other Venetians saw that the Doge's galley was the first to touch down, they all rushed forward and beached their ships . . ."

The Doge's action turned the day. The horrified defenders of Constantinople saw something that they had never believed could happen—a hostile fleet beaching itself under their walls and putting its troops ashore with impunity. (If these walls had indeed been defended by flame-throwers it is inconceivable that they would not have been used at this moment.) The Venetians stormed ashore while, from the ladder-bridges suspended swaying over their heads, other troops dashed in at the level of the walls and jumped on to the parapets.

A general attack was now concentrated on a narrow section of the wall. Scaling ladders were run up against it by the men on the foreshore, while others began to undermine the wall with battering-rams. The demoralised defenders were driven off the parapets, and turned and fled into the city. Within an hour twenty-five of the towers guarding the sea-walls had fallen into Venetian hands. The Doge immediately sent a message to the barons that he had broken into Constantinople, that he had taken the towers, and that nothing could dislodge his men. It was a moment of signal triumph for Dandolo, the fruit of his long planning and of his determination to have his revenge on Constantinople. The barons, disheartened though they were by their own reverses, were overjoyed at the news of the Venetian success. As it turned out, the jubilation of the attackers was premature.

Although the defenders of the sea-wall had broken and fled before the weight of the Venetian onslaught, it was not long before reinforcements began to come up to resist them. "Seeing his foes within the city, the Emperor Alexius began to send his troops against them in ever-increasing numbers. The Venetians were unable to withstand the weight of these attacks and were forced to withdraw. In the process they set fire to the buildings that lay between them and the Greeks . . ." On the inner side of Blachernae, where the houses of workmen and artisans huddled beneath the shelter of the wall, the wooden buildings began to crackle and burst into flame as the Venetians hurled down fire-brands among them. The wind was from the north-east, drawing gently over the Horn, so that the smoke and flames were carried away from the men on the wall, into Blachernae and into the city itself.

There still seemed every likelihood that the Venetians would be able to hold their section of the captured wall, when a message reached the Doge that the Emperor Alexius, with the whole of the imperial army at his back, had come out of the landward gates and was preparing to attack the Crusaders. Robert de Clari described how "The wives and the other ladies of the court came out upon the ramparts to watch the imperial army take up its position . . ." In the face of so great a threat to the Crusaders' camp, and to their own com-paratively small forces, there was nothing that the Doge could do but withdraw his men. It was a bitter moment for Dandolo —his Venetians had not only won a foothold in Constantinople but were holding an important circuit of the seaward walls. But the fate of the whole expedition rested upon a mutual confidence between the Venetian navy and the Crusading army. The Doge knew that he and his men could never capture—let alone hold—Constantinople without the support of the Crusaders. His own galley was the first to leave the shore in front of the walls. He again was the first man to land at the head of the Golden Horn, and to lead his troops to the assistance of the army.

The skirmishes that took place between the Crusaders and the forces under the Emperor Alexius show quite clearly that the Emperor never intended to promote a major engagement. It was enough that, by leading out his troops, he had caused the Venetians to withdraw. The Byzantine army, with its superior numbers, was in a good position to destroy the Crusa-ders in a pitched battle. Either a lack of morale on their part or an unwillingness on the part of the Emperor and his generals to commit them prevented any such event.

It had never at any time been Byzantine policy to sacrifice troops when a successful outcome to an engagement might be achieved by other means. In this respect the Byzantines have often incurred the contempt of western commentators, many of whom, brought up in the warlike tradition of northern Europe, have always in their hearts respected the Spartans more than the Athenians, and the aggressive warrior more than the cultured administrator.

"The Byzantines," writes Professor David Talbot Rice,* "were never a very warlike people. St. Basil had decreed that a soldier who killed should do three years' penance, and though this dictum was soon discarded, the soldier's profession was never a favoured one, nor was death in battle ever considered glorious. Even to fight against the infidel was to be avoided if possible, and the idea of a religious Crusade was something quite foreign to the Byzantine outlook. The endless intrigues and quibbles of Byzantine diplomacy which has so shocked westerners, were often enough the outcome of a genuine desire to avoid bloodshed . . ."

Of what avail in Byzantine eyes was the slaughter of an army if it entailed the decimation of their own? For centuries they had maintained their hold over eastern Europe, and large parts of Asia and North Africa, always as much by diplomacy as by feats of arms. They had seen the barbarians come and go, and they—inheritors of a complex political wisdom—had managed to survive. Only the simple believed that the sword was the sole ruler of the world. Time and again, with a minimum use of arms and a maximum use of statecraft and intelligence, they had seen barbarian invaders disintegrate into mutually hostile tribes.

Their empire was of this world—it was a mercenary trading empire—but at the root of all their thought was Christ's dictum that 'My Kingdom is not of the world'. It is too much to believe that corrupt Byzantine emperors like Alexius were even conscious of such ideas, but they had absorbed the essence of them in the very air that they breathed. Behind its God-guarded walls, the Imperial City, the New Rome, would continue to last (it had always been believed) only so long as God decreed that it should do. The Byzantine grew up with world-weariness in his veins. The marl at the roots of his own city was the body of ancient Rome, and behind him on every headland—from

the Greek Peloponnese to Sicily, North Africa and the Levant—
he saw the whitening bones of temples, fortresses and palaces:
civilisations that had died centuries before his own was born.
To the Byzantine these uncouth Crusaders, who for over a
hundred years had been streaming out of the west to carve
themselves small kingdoms in the east, were as dangerous, and
just as ill-conceived in their opinions, as the Bulgars or the
Turks. They had not been bought off on this occasion, but they
could at least be left to batter themselves into submission against
the unconquerable walls of the city.

The unwillingness of the Byzantine army to commit itself to
a major engagement with the Crusaders could not be put down
solely to demoralisation. Their object was to draw the attackers
away from that section of the city where an unexpected success
had been achieved, and to lure them to make an attack against
the main landward walls. Villehardouin remarks that: "The
Emperor Alexius brought out all his troops by gates which were
about three miles away. So many troops moved out of the city
that you might have believed the whole human race was there
assembled." It is probable that the Emperor himself came out
with the main body of the army from the Golden Gate (which is
about three miles from Blachernae), for at this remove he would
have both space and time to draw up the army at his own
convenience. The Byzantines then moved northward towards
the Crusaders' camp, being joined by other sections of the army
who came out from the other gates on the main circuit of the
walls—from the Second, the Third and the Fourth Military
Gate, the latter just south of the civil gate of St. Romanus.

"When the Venetians came up to support the Crusaders they
said to them: 'We heard that you were engaged against all of
the Greeks. We were worried about the outcome, so we hastened to help you!' The French replied and said: 'Thank God,
we managed things well, for the Emperor did indeed march
out against us—but he did not dare come to close grips.' They
asked the Venetians how things had gone with them, and the
latter replied: 'We made a successful assault, and even got
within the city itself by scaling the walls. We have set fire to the
city and there is no doubt that a great part of it is burned!' "

If the Doge and the barons felt that, on the whole, the day had resulted in nothing more than a reverse, they had at least contrived the ruin of an important part of Constantinople. The fire, sweeping under the north-easterly wind through the quarter of Blachernae, had caused more damage to the city than any previous attack in its long history. Although the palaces and the great houses, the aqueducts, the churches and state buildings were of marble and stone, the houses of ordinary citizens were built of wood. Dried out under the hot July sun, they went up in an incendiary crackle like a forest fire.

As the Crusaders withdrew to their camp "utterly exhausted, and with little to eat or drink", they can have had small confidence in the outcome of the campaign. Although the Byzantine army had apparently been unwilling to engage, the French had been able to see for themselves just how large it was. Although the Venetians had managed for a time to take possession of part of the sea-walls, they had been forced to withdraw—and they would probably have been unable to hold them even if the Crusaders had not asked for their help.

As for the Crusaders themselves, they had had a very unpleasant surprise in their own attack on the barbican at Blachernae. There they had come up against a violent resistance—fair-haired, moustachioed, battleaxe-swinging men, who had driven them back with considerable loss of life. These defenders had shown none of the Byzantine unwillingness to engage in coarse hand-to-hand conflict. It is possible that some of the Crusaders had heard of the Warings before—possible even that among the Norman knights there were some who realised that these formidable opponents were the descendants of those Anglo-Saxons whom King William the Norman had conquered at the Battle of Hastings a century and a half before. The most loyal and hardiest troops among all the polyglot Byzantine army were the Warings—the Varangian guard of the emperors. Whatever others might feel about the Normans and the French, the Warings hated them.

7

THE WARING GUARD

THE Varangian guards, who alone showed themselves faithful to the ancient Roman virtues throughout the events of the Fourth Crusade, were in many respects unique. Other civilisations in the past had used bodies of picked soldiers from foreign countries to defend their rulers, and others were to use them in the future. What distinguished the guards of the Byzantine emperors was the fact that they retained their own language and customs, and their own religious practices. They elected their own officers, and were governed by their own laws. Their commander was known as 'The Leader of the Axe-bearing Guard', or the Acolyte. His title of the Acolyte, or the Follower, was derived from the fact that he always followed immediately behind the Emperor, and stood behind his chair at banquets or his throne on official occasions.

The Turks were later to create a formidable body of warriors in the Janissaries. These were of Christian birth, but were converted Moslems, and were subject to the laws of Islam. The Varangian guards were distinguished from the Janissaries (who would one day occupy a similar position to themselves in the then Turkish city) in that they were free men, obeying their own laws, and—unlike the Janissaries—were never accused of turning against their rulers. Even under weak and corrupt emperors like Alexius III the imperial guard remained faithful and, when required, fought to the death. These men were certainly unusual in the history of mercenaries or 'Foreign Legions'.

They had come to the far end of Europe prepared to fight against any who threatened the sacred person of the Emperor (no matter what his character). Of them it might indeed be said:

> *We can know little (as we care little)*
> *Of the Metropolis: her candled churches,*
> *Her white-gowned pederastic senators,*
> *The cut-throat factions of her Hippodrome,*
> *The eunuchs of her draped saloons . . .*
> *We, not the City, are the Empire's soul:*
> *A rotten tree lives only in its rind.**

The first mention of a Waring guard in Constantinople occurs in 1034. They were reorganised by the Emperor Romanus IV in the mid-eleventh century, and from then on they form a colourful thread in the history of the city. The term Varini or Waring is first found in the Roman historian Tacitus writing in the first century A.D. about the peoples of Germany. It seems to have been used loosely to cover Russians, Swedes, Danes and English, although in Byzantine times it was usually applied to the two latter races.

There is no doubt that after the Norman conquest of England in 1066 a great number of the defeated left their country rather than submit to Norman rule. "When the English had lost their liberty they were eager to find a way of throwing off the yoke of the invader. Some of them, therefore, made their way to Sven, King of the Danes, and urged him to recover the kingdom of his grandfather Canute. Many others went into exile in distant places—some to escape Norman rule, others to make money with the hope of being able one day to return to their homelands. Among the English there were some young men who went far afield and offered their services to the Emperor of Constantinople . . . The English exiles were well received and were used in battle against the Normans, against whom the Greek troops were too weak."* In southern Italy, Sicily, on the Adriatic coastline, and in Asia Minor, the Warings had fought Byzantine battles for over a century, against the steady encroachment of the Normans and the Turks.

After the Norman conquest of England, it certainly appears that a large section of the emperors' guard was English. It has perhaps been forgotten how bitter the 'Old English' felt against the invaders of their island kingdom. The oppressive rule of the Normans undoubtedly led many of the finest Anglo-Saxons to emigrate. The Warings' church in Constantinople was dedicated to SS. Nicolas and Augustine of Canterbury. One contemporary Byzantine historian stated that it was founded by an Englishman who reached Constantinople after the battle of Hastings. Some of the Warings were converted to the Greek Orthodox Faith, but it would seem that most of them still acknowledged the spiritual jurisdiction of Rome. This, however, did not make them any more sympathetic to the Italians, the French or the Normans. It is an interesting thought that, as early as the eleventh century, some of the English should have become wedded to the cause of the Greeks. It was a marriage that would be reaffirmed in the nineteenth century by Byron, and by innumerable Philhellenes since that date.

Usually described as the barbarian guard, or the axe-bearers, the distinctive weapon of the Warings was the Danish battleaxe. It was similar to those used by Harold's troops against the Normans at the Battle of Hastings. Nicetas describes these axes as having only one blade—as opposed to the more familiar double-bladed axe. In the place of the second blade, there was a bayonet-shaped bill. The axe could, therefore, be used for thrusting, as well as for cutting. When wielded by these formidable warriors (most of whom were taller and stronger than the average man), the charge of the Waring guard must have been terrifying even to the battle-hardened Normans. A Byzantine historian, Leo the Deacon, described the appearance of the Waring soldiers. "They have flaxen or reddish hair and blue eyes. They will never be taken in battle, and rather than surrender they will kill themselves." Their hair was worn long on either side of the face, and their beards were distinguished by large moustaches.

Quite apart from their appearance, the Warings must have been curiously incongruous figures at the Greek court of Byzantium, with its Levantine love of subtlety and its oriental love of luxury. Among the bejewelled, silk-clothed nobles and the corruptions of the city, they retained not only the hardihood of the north but something of those other virtues which would one day be allied to the puritan revolution. A contemporary account illustrates their respect for women. A member of the Waring guard had attempted to rape a peasant girl, who had stabbed and killed him while protecting herself. When the matter was investigated by their own officers, the Warings not only exonerated her from any charges but apologised on behalf of their dead comrade. They gave the girl all his property and, to show their disapproval of his action, refused to bury his body. They left it lying above ground, as would have been their custom if a Waring had committed suicide.

It was a curious accident of fate that it should have been the Warings who gave the Normans the fiercest opposition during the Fourth Crusade. These Danes and English had far more in common with the northern Normans (were indeed of the same basic stock) than they had with the Byzantine Greeks, the Pisans or the Anatolians among the rest of the imperial army. They deserve the tribute paid them by a later historian: "No bodyguard in any country was ever more completely trusted than the Varangians. None more completely deserved such trust. They retained their sturdy northern independence in the midst of a corrupt court . . . We may well feel satisfied that the Greek writers repeatedly point out that the emperors found their greatest safety in the spotless loyalty of those among our kinsmen who guarded them, and among whom were many who had left England rather than accept foreign rule."*

The extraordinary thing was that, on the very night after his bodyguard had shown their devotion to him and had routed the Normans, and after an apparent reversal of all the invaders, the Emperor Alexius III decided to make his escape from Constantinople. To the French chroniclers of these events the flight of the Emperor remained a mystery. But to Nicetas, who as a Byzantine nobleman in the city was in a better position to know the truth, the flight of the Emperor was in accord with his whole character: "He was a man without any pride or self-discipline. He was familiar with all, and was extraordinarily soft and weak-spirited. After his crime against his brother, he had been permanently in fear of the day of retribution, and had been greatly disturbed by anxiety and remorse."

Alexius, in fact, had none of the iron qualities needed by tyrants. Having achieved the throne by a plot against his brother, he had shrunk from the logical step of killing both his brother and his brother's son. By merely blinding Isaac and imprisoning him in Blachernae, he had left a dangerous core around which resistance could harden. His gravest error was in allowing his nephew Alexius to escape to Italy. "*Oderint dum metuant!*"—"Let them hate so long as they fear!" However cynical this wisdom, well-known to the ancient Romans, it was something that Alexius as usurper of the throne of New Rome should have learned by heart.

From the moment that the Venetians and the Crusaders had arrived off Constantinople, Alexius III had been meditating flight. Only the exhortations of his relatives, and of those nobles who had aided him to the throne and subsequently benefited by his maladministration, had restrained him. In the meantime, the party which had always secretly supported the blinded Isaac had been growing in strength. Its case was clean-cut and simple—Constantinople and the Empire were threatened only on account of this usurper. Get rid of him, restore Isaac, and all would be well.

The conditions offered by the Doge and the barons were common knowledge. If Isaac's son, Alexius, was made Emperor and Alexius III deposed, the invaders had no further quarrel with the Byzantines. But what need was there to place young Alexius on the throne when his father was still alive? If it was a question of restoring the legitimate Emperor, then it was better surely to bring the blinded Isaac out of the dungeons of Blachernae and place him on his rightful throne. His son could be made Regent if need be, and trained to succeed his father in due course. There can be no doubt that this, or something like it, was the argument that had made itself increasingly felt among certain circles at the Sacred Palace and Blachernae.

On the night of July 17th–18th, 1203, the Emperor Alexius III outwitted his supporters and escaped. As weak and dishonourable in this as in the rest of his life, he deserted his wife

and children. Taking with him only his favourite daughter, the
Princess Irene, and several other women and companions (not
forgetting 10,000 gold pieces and a collection of priceless gems),
he embarked in a ship and slipped southward into the Sea of
Marmora.

8

AN EMPEROR IS CROWNED

"At dawn next day our men began to put on their armour," wrote Villehardouin. "They were already preparing for battle, when the news began to come in from the city..." The Crusaders, who had retired dispirited and exhausted the night before, now learned to their astonishment that the Emperor Alexius had fled.

It is not difficult to imagine how much this news was welcomed. This must surely mean the end of all their troubles. All that remained now (as the Crusaders in their simplicity believed) was to place young Alexius on the throne as Alexius IV, and receive in exchange the money and provisions that he had promised them. Even the dissidents from Corfu must have felt that their difficulties were at an end.

The Doge and the barons can hardly have failed to share in the general enthusiasm. In their possession they had the future emperor of Constantinople, and they were only too happy to restore him to the throne, provided that the promises he had made them were honoured. They could almost anticipate the pleasure that would be felt by the Pope at the result of their expedition. Here was a new emperor who intended to heal the ancient schism between Byzantium and Rome and, by renouncing the heresy of the Orthodox Church, was going to bring the whole of eastern Christendom under the mantle of the Papacy.

"Yet nobody in the camp put much trust in the Greeks..." Already, it would seem, even among Normans and French (unfamiliar with the humid Byzantine climate) a certain element of mistrust had begun to occur. They were not to be disillusioned

—in their suspicions, at any rate. Hardly had the cheers died down from the news that Alexius III had abdicated than they learned that the Byzantines had already circumvented them.

Early that morning, as soon as the flight of Alexius had been confirmed, the party in favour of the ex-Emperor had gone down to the dungeons of Blachernae. There they had found the blinded and enfeebled Isaac. They had hastily brought him up into the daylight, clothed him in the imperial robes and installed him as emperor. Now they sent word to the Doge and the leaders of the Crusade that their real emperor was restored.

It is not difficult to imagine the frustration felt by the Doge and his fellow-conspirators. They were on the very eve of success—only to learn that these wily Byzantines had outwitted them, and in a way that they had never expected. In all the discussions in Venice, Zara and Corfu about the aims of the expedition, no mention had ever been made of the deposed Emperor. Perhaps the Doge and his companions had assumed that Isaac was dead. If not, perhaps they had convinced themselves that he would be swiftly disposed of once the claims of his son were made known.

They had counted on placing young Alexius upon the throne, and they had assured the simple Crusaders that in helping to do this they were rectifying a grave wrong. But what argument could they produce against the restoration to the throne of the very man who had been deprived of it, who had been blinded by the usurper and who had lived for the past eight years in the imperial dungeons? Their case for staying in Byzantine territory could only rest upon one thing—that they had brought their fleet and army thus far north on the definite understanding that they would be paid for their services. Everything depended upon this. If Isaac was prepared to confirm the guarantees given by his son, then it would have seemed impossible for the Crusaders to do anything but take their money and go.

Accordingly a deputation was arranged to enter the city, find out the exact circumstances of Isaac's restoration and demand the fulfilment of his son's promises. Once this had been done, the barons were prepared to allow Alexius to enter the city and meet his father. They were certainly determined that the only Byzantine guarantor of the agreement should not be allowed into Constantinople at this juncture—possibly to close the gates against them and renounce his pledges.

Geoffrey de Villehardouin and Matthew de Montmorency, together with two Venetians selected by the Doge, were chosen as ambassadors. The four men were conducted to the walls of Blachernae and the great gate began to open. "As soon as it was opened, they dismounted from their horses. Now they saw that the Greeks had stationed the Danes and English, with their battleaxes in hand, along the whole route from the gate to the palace of Blachernae itself. And when they reached the palace they found the Emperor Isaac arrayed in such dazzling robes that it is almost impossible to describe them. Beside him sat the Empress, a very beautiful woman, the daughter of the King of Hungary. Gathered together round them were so many noblemen and their ladies that there was hardly room to move. (All those who yesterday had been the enemies of the Emperor Isaac had now become the most ingratiating of friends.)"

The formality and grandeur of the Byzantine court eclipsed anything that could be found in Europe. An immense complexity and richness in court ritual was part of the imperial tradition. It had been used throughout the centuries to overawe visiting ambassadors, kings and nobles—whether they came from Europe, from Russia or from Asia Minor and the East. The Byzantines were well aware of the importance of first impressions. They were well aware, too, that foreign visitors from whatever land they came, had never seen anything to equal the magnificence of Constantinople's architecture, nor the pomp and circumstance that surrounded God's Vice-Regent.

The Sultan of the Seljuk Turks, Arslan II, who visited the city some fifty years before these events, had been so overawed by the glamour of the court that, although invited to do so, he had never had the courage to sit beside the Emperor. His food and refreshments were sent daily to his quarters in vessels of silver and gold—which no one ever bothered to reclaim. In the Sacred Palace itself, far more than in Blachernae, everything was designed to reduce the visitor to a feeling of his own insignificance. The Emperor, clad in his bejewelled and gold-embroidered robes, would receive him seated on the golden throne, while all around him the chief ministers and court officials moved like enamelled flowers in some hieratic procession. Near the throne stood the famous golden plane tree on which mechanical birds moved their wings and sang, while the golden lions and gryphons on either side of the throne opened their mouths and roared. At a given moment, as the visitor was prostrating himself in reverence, the notes of an organ would peal out and the golden throne would whirl aloft, disappearing behind draperies hung from the ceiling. A few minutes later the throne would slowly descend, with the Emperor in a completely new but equally magnificent suit of robes.

But even if the French and Venetian ambassadors on this occasion were not treated to so pyrotechnic a display, there is no doubt from the tone of Villehardouin's account that they were profoundly impressed. The walls of polychrome marble in Blachernae palace might not compare with the Sacred Palace itself, but they were infinitely grander and more imposing than anything known at the time in western Europe. Bronze fountains spouted water, the ceilings gleamed with golden tesserae, and everywhere there were mosaics of incredible splendour. An eleventh-century Byzantine poem describes the innumerable classical themes used by the mosaic artists: Achilles and Agamemnon; Ulysses defying the Cyclops; and, above all, the feats of the great Alexander, the first man to establish a Greek Empire in the East.*

One thing that must have impressed the Crusaders, no matter what their rank, was the culture and education of the Byzantines. While even important nobles such as Villehardouin himself were scarcely literate, for the skills of reading and writing they left to their priests,* their Byzantine equivalents were conversant with the Greco-Roman culture upon which their civilisation was based. Women, too, were among the most accomplished citizens in Constantinople. A well-known story dating from the eleventh century illustrates the sophistication of the Byzantine world. The Emperor Constantine IX was on his way to the Hippodrome in company with his Caucasian mistress, Skleraina. One of the attendant courtiers remarked: "ὀυ νέμεσις" (It is no shame). The courtier was quoting from that passage in the Iliad where the old men, looking at Helen as she walked on the walls of Troy, remarked: "It is no shame to fight for such as she!" These two words from Homer were at once recognised, and their appositeness approved by the courtiers of Constantinople. This was at a time in the Middle Ages when most of Europe was uncultured and illiterate.

Throughout the many encounters that were to take place during the next months between the leaders of the Crusaders and the Byzantines, it is noticeable that the former—while despising the citizens of Constantinople—seem constantly uneasy in their presence. Indeed something of the violence of the tragedy that was to overwhelm the city may perhaps be traced to this very fact. No man likes to be made aware that he is culturally and educationally inferior to those whom he regards as weaker than himself. The Crusaders were aware that they were stronger, even perhaps that they represented a more vigorous society. But, like that phenomenon of other days, the rough private soldier of a 'liberating army' who is billeted in a castle full of priceless treasures, they felt aware of their own inadequacy.

The Emperor Isaac, blinded and old though he was, seemed transformed into another being. Far from having to deal with an ex-prisoner overjoyed at his release and eager to welcome his liberators, the ambassadors found that they were face to face with the representative of all the imperial past. This was the ruler who was Caesar and Pope in one, the Autokrator.

Villehardouin spoke on behalf of the delegation. "Sire," he said, "you are no doubt aware of the service we have rendered your son. We for our part have kept the terms of our agreement with him. But we cannot, in all fairness, allow him to return to the city until we have some guarantee for his part of the agreement. Your son therefore beseeches you to confirm the treaty between us on exactly the same terms that he has made."

Isaac inquired what the terms were. He was told that Alexius had agreed, first of all, to place the whole Empire under obedience to the spiritual jurisdiction of Rome. Secondly, to supply the army with 200,000 silver marks and a year's provisions. Thirdly, to send 10,000 troops in his own ships to help the Crusaders in Egypt, and fourthly to keep them there at his own charge for a whole year. Lastly, he had agreed to maintain throughout his life, and at his own expense, a force of 500 knights in Outremer, or 'the Land Overseas', as the Holy Land and the Crusader territories of the Levant were known.

Isaac, released only a few hours from his dungeon in Blachernae and so suddenly restored to the scarlet buskins and imperial mantle of Constantinople, revealed that his eyesight might be gone, but not his brain. "You ask a great deal of us," he replied, "more I think than we can possibly perform. However, I realise how much both I and my son owe to you—indeed, if I were to give you the whole empire it would be no more than enough." A certain irony was evident in his words. Yet there was clearly nothing he could do at that moment but ratify the treaty that his son had made. Villehardouin, de Montmorency, and the two Venetians spurred back to their camp. Happily they held aloft the document ratified by the Emperor, with his golden seal set upon it.

On July 19th, father and son were reunited.. The gates of the city were opened wide in peace, and it might have seemed that once again in the long history of the Empire all would end well. The lights shone out from the palace of Blachernae, there was feasting and rejoicing both in the court and in the camp of the Crusaders.

Beneath this surface cheerfulness there lay an ocean of despair. Almost everything that Alexius had so glibly promised could not be fulfilled. The treasury was depleted by his uncle Alexius III (not only in his flight but in his years of misrule). The whole Empire indeed had been drained dry by a succession of indifferent emperors—not least the blinded Isaac—as well as by the steady decline in Byzantine fortunes ever since the battle of Manzikert in 1071, when the Turks had begun to establish their dominion over Asia Minor. One of the sharper

rocks upon which everything was to founder was the promise
of Alexius, now ratified by his father, that the Greek Church
would accept the jurisdiction of Rome.

The whole essence of the Byzantine Empire and the God-
guarded city of Constantinople was a spiritual one. It was here
that Constantine the Great had established the 'New Rome'
when the old Rome had ceased to be the heart of the Roman
Empire. In the eyes of its inhabitants the city was the true home
of the Christian faith, and indeed its Asia Minor territories—
so many of them now lost to the Seljuk Turks—had been the
first Christianised areas in the world. The great Emperor
Justinian had defined the position of Church and state in his
Laws: "Two gifts are bestowed by God upon men: the priesthood and the imperial authority. The former is concerned with
divine matters, the latter with human. Both have their same
origin and both adorn human life. Nothing is of more importance to the Emperor than that he should support the priesthood, so that the priests in their turn may pray God to aid the
Emperor."

Church and state were interwoven in Byzantine society. It
was a theocratic world, in which the ruler was priest as well as
king. The barbarian invasions which had isolated Rome in the
seventh century A.D. had left the mainstream of Christian theo-
logy in the hands of the eastern empire. Rome had developed
quite separately since that time, had evolved among other
things the conception of Papal supremacy. The Greek Church
had always been more inclined towards mysticism than the
Roman. Christianity was an eastern religion, and it is hardly
surprising that the Byzantines felt themselves to be more in
accord with the traditions of the early fathers of the Church
than western Europeans. For centuries now they had defended
the Faith against all pagan invaders (even at a time when Rome
itself was occupied by them). To be told that they must now
submit themselves to the overlordship of Rome, and to an
acceptance of various points of dogma with which they had long
disagreed, was to ask the impossible.

In view of the difficulties that lay in the way of fulfilling their
promises to the Crusaders and the Venetians, it is not surprising

that Isaac and his son Alexius should have wanted as long a respite as possible. They needed to think things over and to decide how best to meet (or avoid) their obligations. One of the first requests they made to the barons was that the army should withdraw from the area of the city and return to the northern side of the Golden Horn. Isaac was careful to explain that he was afraid of trouble breaking out between his own citizens and the troops. The Crusaders and Venetians agreed, and "pitched their camp on the far side of the harbour, where they lived in peace and plenty . . .".

The real problem that troubled the inner circle of the Crusaders was that they had suddenly found themselves faced with the apparition of the blinded Emperor. Even though Isaac had now agreed to all their demands, they felt uneasy unless their chosen instrument was formally made emperor. In the course of ten days' constant wrangling and argument, they and the Byzantines managed to come to a most unusual agreement— Alexius and his father should be jointly crowned. In fact, the nobles and courtiers of Constantinople had almost as little right in insisting upon Isaac being made emperor as the Crusaders had in proposing the claim of his son. If the idea of a regular dynastic succession was foreign in principle to Constantinople, it was also an accepted fact that a blind or otherwise disabled man could never be emperor.

On August 1st, 1203, Alexius and his father Isaac were crowned together in Santa Sophia. "Shortly afterwards," says Villehardouin, "the new emperor began to discharge the debt that he owed the army . . ." It is noticeable that he refers only to Alexius, now Alexius IV, and makes no mention of his father the co-Emperor. But to discharge so large a debt, far more than was readily available in the imperial treasury, Alexius was forced to that resort of all indigent rulers in the early days of economics —melting down all available objects of precious metal. "Even the churches were profaned," Nicetas tells us, "and the holy images were stripped of their ornaments. The consecrated vessels were carried off to satisfy the rapacity of the Latins." Thus began the spoliation of Constantinople's art treasures. Enamelled ikons were melted down, gems were stripped from

their settings and centuries-old ornaments of gold and silver
were carried off to the treasurers of the Crusaders and the
Venetians.

Throughout these weeks the people of Constantinople were
silent. The abdication of Alexius III, the restoration of Isaac,
the co-emperorship with his son—these events seem to have
meant little to them. The nobles and the priests might be
concerned by what was happening in the palace, the one on
account of their money and position, and the other on account
of the threat to their Faith. But to ordinary citizens such events
signified very little, provided that life resumed its normal terms,
that trade with the outside world began again and that the
threat to their city from this foreign army was removed. One
thing only disturbed them—the sudden demands of the imperial tax-gatherers. That they should now be forced to contribute large sums in order to get rid of these invaders (who had
restored an emperor no better than the one who had fled) was
more than they were willing to endure without any protest.

Every day incidents multiplied between the citizens of
Constantinople and the troops. The Crusaders crossed over
from Galata in their thousands to eat, drink, buy and stare in
dumb wonder at the buildings, the bustling streets and the giant
aqueducts and the lofty walls. The citizens liked neither their
manners nor their presence in the city.

Alexius IV was only too soon made aware that not only the
citizens but many in the court, were hostile to him. His father
was enfeebled by his years in captivity and incapable of taking
an active part in administration. But Alexius could not feel
himself master in his own house while his father was, technically
at least, his partner. At the moment his inheritance was heavily
mortgaged to the Venetians and the Crusaders, but he was
uncomfortably aware that it was only in this quarter that any
real support for him existed. It was not surprising that he took
to frequenting their camp. He found companions among the
Crusaders and even, so he believed, friends. His behaviour
disgusted the Byzantines: "He disgraced the imperial purple.
Frequently he went to the camp of the barbarians [The Crusa-
ders] and spent whole days there in gambling and debauchery.

One day his companions even snatched the gold crown from his head and replaced it with a woollen cap . . ." Nicetas, lover and historian of the ancient splendours and virtues of his city, could not help but lament the state to which it had fallen. Was this the heir to Constantine, to Justinian, to Basil the Bulgar-Slayer and to all the centuries of imperial might—this drunken boy allowing loutish Franks to mock the sacred crown?

Alexius confessed to the barons that there was a large party in Constantinople who did not view his accession to the throne with any pleasure. As he told the Doge and the inner council: "There are many who show me a fair countenance but do not love me. The Greeks cannot forget that it is only through you that I have recovered my inheritance. I know that the association between you and the Venetians lasts only until Michaelmas, and that you will then be leaving. This is so short a space of time that it does not permit me to fulfil my obligations to you. And the Greeks hate me so much on your account that if you leave I shall surely lose both my empire and my life . . ." He went on to make them a proposition.

"Stay here until March, I beg you. I am prepared to pay your fleet for a further year from this Michaelmas, and I will supply your army with all you need until Easter. By that time I shall have my government so firmly established that there will be no danger of my losing my empire. My revenues will have come in and I shall be able to discharge my debt to you. I shall also have equipped a fleet so that I can either go with you myself, or send them with you as we have already agreed. For your part, you will have the whole of next summer in which to conduct your campaign against the Saracens."

Alexius was in the usual unhappy position of a gambler who cannot meet his debts. He was confident that, given time, he would not only be able to satisfy his creditors but would also be financially secure himself. How little he knew of the exhausted state of the exchequer of Constantinople is evident from his words. Is it possible he could have believed that his people would not only shoulder the current burden of taxation but would accept even more (for that was what his new guarantees would certainly mean)?

One man who must have been pleased by Alexius' words (may possibly even have suggested them as a solution of his difficulties) was Enrico Dandolo. Bearing in mind the relationship between Venice and Egypt, the Doge can never have had any intention of allowing the Crusade to proceed. He had checked it in Venice itself, diverted it successfully to Zara, had held it together by ingenious emotional blackmail in Corfu and had then most successfully of all diverted it to Constantinople. As he knew well enough, the capture of Zara and the elimination of this threat to the Venetian trade-route in the Adriatic was worth more than the Crusaders had ever owed him. But the lack of saleable plunder in Zara had enabled him to maintain that their debt was still undischarged.

It is impossible to calculate how much he and the Venetians had gained already in coin and treasure, but there can be little doubt that their books showed the Crusaders still deeply in debt. His fleet had stormed the famous defences of the Golden Horn and now rode securely at anchor inside its sheltered waters. Autumn was coming on. Indeed, within a few weeks the temperate summer winds would cease to blow and the irregular gales of winter would set in. That would be no time to take a large fleet through the treacherous waters of the Aegean, all the way to the shores of Egypt. The Doge perhaps had always anticipated that, once he had contrived to get the Crusaders hundreds of miles north of their objective, he would be able to arrange his own terms for their return.

The original plot entered into by the Doge, Boniface of Montferrat and Philip of Swabia was to place young Alexius upon the throne, and to break the power of the Byzantine Empire. As a sop to Pope Innocent III they were going to toss him the subjection of the whole of this heretic community to the See of Rome. Dandolo, however, had always been interested in the acquisition of the trade of the eastern empire. Venice had been active in Levantine seas for many years and had often been in conflict with the navy and the mercantile interests of this old-established power. As a practical man it was the trade in which he was concerned; in the islands of the Aegean, in the land-route that passed through Constantinople

from Asia, in the island of Crete and in all the potential wealth
that might well accrue to his own city rather than to Constantinople.

Confident that Alexius was little more than a puppet, the
Doge was only too happy at the prospect of keeping the army
and the fleet at Constantinople throughout the winter. The
main problem was to see that Alexius' suggestion was presented
to the Crusaders in such a way that they would be willing yet
again to forsake their Crusading oath, and stay encamped
on Christian territory rather than proceed against the infidel.

When the Emperor's proposals were put to the army it was
hardly surprising that "they gave rise to great discord, just as
much as on the previous occasions". The party who had been
promised at Corfu that, if they would stay with the rest until
Michaelmas, they would then be given ships to transport them
to Syria were rightly infuriated. Villehardouin, anxious as ever
to place the blame anywhere but where it really rested, calls
them "the party who wished to see the dissolution of the army".
They were, in fact, no more than the party who wanted to get
on with the task for which they had joined the Crusade. "Give
us the ships to take us to Syria," they cried, "Let us go as you
promised that you would!"

But, just as the plotters had earlier conjectured, circumstances
were now very much against the pro-Syria party. Some of their
number had already reconciled themselves to the idea of spend-
ing the winter in Constantinople, some had lost any enthusiasm
for the Crusade, and all of them were dependent on the Venetians for their transport. It was not so difficult this time to
reconcile them to yet another delay. It was quickly pointed out
that "if we sail now we shall arrive in Syria at the beginning of
winter and it will be impossible to commence the campaign.
Better far to wait until March, see this emperor safely established
on his throne, and leave with plenty of money and provisions."

The die was cast. The Doge and the inner council of the
barons were happy to inform Alexius that they agreed to his
proposals. They would stay in the city until the spring, and in

return they looked to him to fulfil his part of the bargain. "Thus, with the help of Almighty God, the matter was favourably terminated. The Venetians confirmed on oath that they would hold their fleet at our disposal for a further year from Michaelmas, and the Emperor Alexius paid the fleet as he had promised."

9

THE GREAT FIRE

THE autumn and winter of 1203 were harsh and bitter for the citizens of Constantinople. It was not the first time in their history that they had had a foreign army encamped outside their walls, but it was the first time that the invaders had been encouraged to come inside them. Swaggering through the streets in their chain-mail, the knights and men-at-arms marvelled—and despised. Unable to speak Greek themselves, they felt that these foreigners should at least have been educated to speak French or Italian. Unable to understand a far older and more sophisticated civilisation, they were sure that these gowned and perfumed citizens were all effeminate. It is part of a soldier's nature to despise civilians—but how much the more he despises the civilians of a foreign country.

During that autumn, part of the Crusading army accompanied the Emperor Alexius on an expedition through the neighbouring region of Thrace. "Alexius himself had said to the barons that he owned no more than Constantinople and that he would be very short of money if this was his only possession. His uncle was still the ruler of all the other cities and castles which ought to be his. He asked the barons, therefore, to help him establish control over the neighbouring country, saying that he would willingly give them some profit out of it . . ."

The idea of taking the young Emperor away from the city appealed to the Doge and to Boniface of Montferrat. It was sensible to ensure that the towns and garrisons of Thrace recognised their new emperor, for it was from them that much of the money would have to be raised to pay his debts. There was also the chance that they might run the ex-Emperor Alexius

III to ground, for so long as he was at liberty there was always the danger of a counter-revolution being made against the present ruler from the provinces.* Rumour had it that Alexius III was in the great fortress city of Adrianople in northern Thrace. An additional reason, and indeed the most important one, for getting the young Alexius away from the city was that there was every likelihood that he would be seduced from his allegiance to the Crusaders and Venetians by patriotic elements in the court.

The two figures who emerge as active in their resistance to the invaders are Theodore Lascaris and Alexius Ducas. Both were sons-in-law of Alexius III and both, therefore, had no reason to like either Isaac or his son, the new Emperor Alexius IV. Theodore Lascaris had already shown his mettle during the first skirmishes outside the city and had attempted, though unsuccessfully, to put some spirit into his father-in-law. After the latter's flight, however, he seems to have become temporarily discouraged and to have withdrawn from public affairs. His time would yet come.

Alexius Ducas, nicknamed Murtzuphlus because his eyebrows met in the middle, was the principal influence among the patriots and nationalists. Murtzuphlus was a pragmatic patriot who desired to see the foreigners out of Byzantine territory, but who realised that the best way to achieve this was to appear to be friendly with them. To this end he cultivated Alexius IV and won his way into the Emperor's favour, being made *Protovestiarius* or Chief of the Imperial Wardrobe and Private Treasury. This was not only an important position in the state but one that brought him daily into close contact with the Emperor.

It is clear that both the Doge and Boniface recognised an enemy to their cause in this bushy-eyebrowed son-in-law of the ex-Emperor. The sooner that Alexius could be removed from his influence, and of others of his persuasion, the better it would be for the Crusaders and the Venetians. Accordingly, a number of the leading barons, including the Marquis of Montferrat, took nearly half the army and set off as escort to the Emperor. Their intention was to reduce any cities that might refuse to acknowledge the new ruler, and to accept the allegiance of all his other subjects.

Alexius and his troops were away from the city for nearly three months, "conquering twenty cities and forty castles", according to de Clari. Villehardouin, however, maintains that all the Greeks on either side of the Bosphorus willingly paid him allegiance as their rightful lord. (The only exception was the King of Wallachia and Hungaria to the north, who had sometime since established an almost independent state.)

It was during the absence of Alexius and the Marquis of Montferrat that the troubles in the city came to a head. Not a day passed without some brawl in the streets, some insult exchanged between Greek and Latin, or some drunken disturbance such as soldiers have always made when billeted in foreign countries. The hatred of the Byzantines for these Frankish invaders was repressed only by fear of their military strength and of the Venetian fleet.

It was by the Venetians and, by a simple corollary, all Italians, that the Byzantines felt most affronted. There had been Italian colonies in Constantinople for a long time, and indeed throughout the Empire. The Byzantines were not by nature xenophobic people—indeed they were an amalgam of nations somewhat similar to the modern United States. They had always been willing to accept merchants and craftsmen from other countries into their cities and dominions. The result was that there was a large colony of Pisans established in Constantinople itself, while many Genoese and Venetians had settled in the suburb of Galata across the Goldern Horn. Throughout the fifty years or so before the Fourth Crusade, the power and influence of these foreign colonies had been steadily increasing. But whereas the Empire had been rich enough in the past to accept foreign traders without loss to itself or its native citizens, the position had changed greatly during the latter years of the twelfth century. The Byzantines had permitted foreign colonies to settle but had not assimilated them, with the result that the colonists' loyalties were to their own native countries. A growing resentment against foreigners, therefore, was sure to arise among the native artisans and merchants as soon as their own fortunes dwindled. By 1203 it needed very little to spark this into life—let alone the presence of an invading army composed of co-religionists of the foreign colonists.

The incident that led to the calamitous fire of Constantinople—a fire that far eclipsed the one that had been started by the Venetians during their assault on the walls—was typical of the disturbed state of the city. "A party of drunken Franks," says Nicetas, "undertook, when in their cups, to destroy the mosque of the Saracens. In the course of the brawl that followed (for the Greeks helped the Saracens to defend their property against the Latins) the city was set on fire."

The fact that there should be a mosque frequented by Saracens in a Christian city had infuriated the Crusaders. They were incapable of realising that, just as the Byzantines tolerated Italian colonies of traders in their territory, so they allowed trade in the Empire between 'infidels' from the East and their own merchants. Constantinople had not survived for so many centuries by being a city of intolerance.

The Byzantines had fought the Turks for many years, but only because the Turks were attacking their empire. The idea of a Crusading mission against all the heathen was totally foreign to the Byzantine understanding of history. They had learned over many centuries that force of arms was not enough to make converts. In their long experience of the East they had noted that the followers of Mahomet were in many respects more tolerant than the Christians from Outremer. For themselves they were convinced of the sanctity and truth of the Christian Faith, but they recognised that they had to live—and survive—in an imperfect world.

It was this attitude of the Byzantines which had made both the city and its people disliked and distrusted by Crusading armies. Imbued with their militant conception of Christianity, they could only regard the Byzantines and their Church as backsliders, weak in the Faith, and cowardly in the face of its enemies. It was beyond their intelligence, or the statecraft of their rulers, to understand that the Byzantine Empire was the best and only shield for Europe against the forces of the East. Fired as they were by their preachers and by Papal ambitions,

they could not understand that only by some element of tolerance, and by finding a *modus vivendi* with the races professing
Islam, could the Christian world maintain its necessary eastern
connections and survive.

The Mosque which was pillaged and sacked by a group of
Flemish, Venetians and Pisans stood in the city itself between
the Church of Saint Irene and the Golden Horn. It was north
of St. Irene (itself a little north of Santa Sophia) and the quarter
of the Saracen traders abutted on the Horn—right next to that
of the Pisans, a little farther to the west. There can be no doubt
that the Pisans had for a long time disliked the proximity of
these Saracen traders, and that they found an admirable
opportunity for venting their dislike of them under the protection of Crusading swords.

The Pisans furthermore had a current grievance against the
citizens of Constantinople. Their own quarter had been
attacked and pillaged by the Byzantine mob shortly after the
arrival of the Crusaders. The people had somewhat naturally
associated this invading Latin army with the presence in their
midst of Italian merchants, who subscribed to the doctrines of
Rome and spoke the same language as the Venetians. The
result of all this was that the Pisans, having suffered at the
hands of the Greeks saw an admirable opportunity of making
good their own losses from the Saracen traders whose activities
had long conflicted with their own.

Finding the Saracens at prayer in their mosque, "they sacked
it and took away much priceless treasure". It was at this point
that Greek citizens joined the fray, as much to attack the hated
Latins as to protect the Saracens. Somehow or other a fire
broke out during the brawl—a fire that, as Nicetas tells us,
"surpassed any that had ever previously occurred in the city".

Fanned by a brisk northerly wind, the fire swept southward.
The sparks and flying debris blown from the wooden houses
swirled across the gaps of streets. The flames leaped right over
Mesé (Middle) Street and engulfed one of the richest sections
of the city. Mesé Street was the most important thoroughfare
in Constantinople, and ran right through its heart from the
Gate of Charisius in the western wall to the great Forum of

Theodosius, the Hippodrome and finally to Santa Sophia
itself. Acre upon acre of wooden houses were consumed, and
the intense heat was too much even for stone and marble.

The Crusaders on the far side of the Golden Horn "were overcome with grief as they watched great churches and palaces
sinking in ashes to the ground. The broad streets where the
rich merchants and shopkeepers lived were swallowed up in the
inferno. The fire ran right from the harbour through the most
crowded part of the city, finally reaching the Sea of Marmora
on the far side, and sweeping close to the cathedral of Santa
Sophia itself . . ." It lasted for eight days, Villehardouin tells us,
and at its peak cut a swathe over three miles wide through the
heart of Constantinople. Hundreds of men, women and children were burned to death, thousands more lost their homes and
possessions, and the city itself received the worst blow that had
ever befallen it.*

The great fire marked the end of any reasonable relations
between the citizens and the Crusaders. From now on the
people of Constantinople were so distraught and incensed that
no Latin was safe within the walls. Whatever may have been
the initial cause of the fire, there could be no doubt in the minds
of the Byzantines that, but for the invaders, this terrible blow
would never have befallen them. Franks, Genoese, Pisans,
Venetians were equally condemned and "none of the Latins
who had previously lived in Constantinople dared to stay in the
city". They fled across the Golden Horn with their wives and
children, and took refuge either in the camp of the Crusaders
or among the other foreign colonies in Galata. Over 15,000
refugees were added to the numbers on the far side of the
harbour. The lines of division were now clearly laid down:
Crusaders, Venetians and foreign colonists on the one side;
Greeks on the other.

This was the situation when, on November 11th, 1203,
Alexius IV, in company with the Marquis of Montferrat and
the other half of the army, returned to the city. A large part of
Constantinople lay in ruins and open hostilities had broken out
between the citizens and all foreigners. Yet still Alexius must
find the means to discharge his debts.

He retired to the palace at Blachernae. It was not long before the influences that the Doge had mistrusted began to make themselves felt. Murtzuphlus and his party could sense that the temper of the citizens was with them. They could feel the rising tide of indignation. They knew that further demands for money and increased taxation would provide the spark for an uprising.

While the blinded Isaac was still in theory co-emperor, he seems to have been almost equally disregarded by both court and Crusaders. Falling prey to the superstitions that were in the very air of Constantinople, he spent more and more of his time in the company of monks, priests and astrologers. Alexius, for his part, seems to have returned from the expedition curiously ignorant of his true position, and full of an unmerited self-confidence. The attention paid to him by the Marquis of Montferrat and the other barons, the evidence throughout his recent journey that most of his subjects were prepared to accept him as emperor, these together with his undoubted possession of the throne blinded him to the true facts. He was still emperor only upon the sufferance of the Crusaders and, in the final analysis, of his own people. The former would tolerate him only so long as he discharged his debts, and the latter (although he did not fully realise it) viewed him as the author of all their misfortunes.

Everything revolved around the question of money—as indeed it had done ever since the Crusaders had entered into their misguided contract with the Venetians. Alexius had promised at Zara to pay 400,000 marks if the Crusaders would set him upon the throne. Immediately after the coronation he seems to have paid about a quarter of this sum, but this had exhausted the immediate resources of his treasury. Since then he had been making further small payments as and when revenues came in, or by dint of melting down church plate and other ornaments. He had laid a further burden of debt at his door when he had persuaded the army and the fleet to stay in Constantinople until the spring.

As the Doge must have anticipated, the regular payment of the sum Alexius had contracted for was quite beyond his

powers. This was entirely to Dandolo's satisfaction, for he had
no intention of allowing the army to proceed until his objective
had been achieved. Neither he, nor Philip of Swabia, nor
Boniface of Montferrat had any interest in the Crusade as such.
The Doge wished to bring about the destruction of the Byzantine Empire for the benefit of Venice, and Boniface most probably envisaged himself as the new Emperor of Constantinople.
Philip of Swabia, far away in Germany, was interested pri-
marily in the discomfiture of the Pope, and in securing his own
position as Emperor of the West. He had restored his father-
in-law Isaac, and his brother-in-law Alexius, to the throne, and
it seems likely that his own interests in Constantinople were now
satisfied.

Only the Doge knew exactly what he wanted; only the Doge
had the means of bringing Alexius to the ground. Robert de
Clari tells a story which is suspect only because it is unlikely
that he would have been present to overhear the discussion
concerned. It is interesting, however, as indicating the type of
tale which was going the rounds of the army, and it illustrates
the general feeling among the Crusaders about the relationship
between Alexius IV and Doge Dandolo. After the payments
began to dwindle, and after innumerable representations had
been made to Alexius IV to discharge his debts as quickly as
possible, a meeting was arranged between him and Dandolo.
The latter had himself rowed across the Horn in a galley with
three other galleys as escort, while Alexius IV came down on
horseback to meet him outside Blachernae. Dandolo, according to de Clari, immediately said to him: "Alexius, what do you
think you are doing? Don't forget that we lifted you out of your
pitiable condition, and that we made you emperor and had you
crowned. Why don't you keep your promises and discharge
your debts to us?" Alexius replied: "No. I have no intention
of doing any more than I have done already!" "Haven't you?"
said the Doge. "Why you stupid youth, we dragged you out
of the shit! We'll soon enough put you back in the shit! Just
bear this in mind—I'll do everything I can to see that you're
completely ruined!"

But the long winter had set in before things reached such a

total impasse. Constantinople is cold in winter, and the condition of the army was an unhappy one, encamped on the northern side of the Golden Horn and unable to visit the city and buy provisions. It was hardly surprising that bands of soldiers began to ransack the countryside. The summer villas of Byzantine nobles were plundered, and neighbouring churches were looted. Ever since the great fire the citizens of Constantinople had been in a state of undeclared war with the invaders. Ever since the return of Alexius, he had been delaying more and more in the payments of his debts, and had been listening to the advice of Murtzuphlus and the patriotic party that he should have no further dealings with the foreigners. "The Franks have been paid quite enough!" was the refrain that was constantly in his ears.

Weak and irresolute, having achieved his throne by foreign intervention, and now aware of the hatred of his people, Alexius could only hope that if hostilities were to begin, the walls of the city would save him just as they had saved so many others in the past. His father, meanwhile, sunk in sickness and superstition, listened only to the voices of the past. Like many Byzantines he had a weakness for astrologers and it was on their advice that he had the statue of the Calydonian Boar dragged from the Hippodrome into the Sacred Palace. This classical statue of the legendary beast that had once ravaged the Aetolian region of Greece commemorated, as it were, the forces of violence and barbarism. It was the belief of the astrologers that with its help the equally violent and barbaric Crusaders might be overthrown. Meanwhile Alexius Ducas, or Murtzuphlus 'the bushy-eyebrowed one', bided his time. He, too, believed in violence, but in violence applied with skill and intelligence.

IO

MURTZUPHLUS SEIZES POWER

TOWARDS the end of the year 1203 the Doge and the barons
decided on one last formal appeal to Alexius. His payments to
them had been growing steadily smaller and more irregular,
until at last they had ceased altogether. It was essential that
the army, no less than the fleet, should know where it stood, and
whether the Emperor intended to fulfil his obligations. The
Crusaders' position was growing increasingly difficult as the
wintry weather set in.

Three Crusaders and three Venetians were chosen as
ambassadors, an equal division as on the previous occasion,
and Conon de Béthune was again made principal spokesman.
It is hardly surprising to find that Geoffrey de Villehardouin
was one of the three ambassadors chosen from the Crusaders,
for he seems to have been nearly always selected by the inner
council to represent their interests. There can be little doubt,
after reading his history of the Fourth Crusade, that Villehardouin—like so many military men throughout the centuries—was as gullible as he was brave. His straightforward
presentation of the facts (as he was told them) was enough to
make even the opposition doubt their arguments. His sincerity
was a useful cover for the duplicity of others.

The ambassadors arrived at Blachernae and were received
by Alexius and his father Isaac. Conon de Béthune now delivered his prepared speech. He reminded Alexius and his
father that they had both agreed to discharge their debts to the
Crusaders and the Venetians—and that they were failing to do
so.

"If you only fulfil what you have promised," he went on,

"everything will be well. But I must tell you that if you renegue on these promises the Crusaders will have no more to do with you under any circumstances whatsoever. They command me to tell you that they will never begin hostilities without due warning. It is not the custom in their countries to act treacherously . . ." Conon de Béthune meant by this no more than that the army would not make open war without some blatant act of aggression—such as would be instantly recognisable as a challenge. It is interesting to see that at this late juncture the Crusaders were preparing to observe the so-called 'Laws of Chivalry', which they had notably dispensed with since their departure from Corfu.

In the palace, where protocol had been regarded for so many centuries as of the utmost importance, the ambassadors' statement was received with astonishment. The Greeks were not only surprised but disgusted by such a rough and blatant disregard of formal etiquette. These Franks were actually threatening the Emperor in the presence of all the court. "No one before had ever dared to issue a challenge to the Emperor of Constantinople in his very own palace! Alexius himself and all the other nobles of the court showed their displeasure by their unsmiling faces . . ."

The simple Westerners had failed to realise that in the Levant one does not treat attempts to deceive or evade responsibility in such a bluff and downright manner. Constantinople was oriental in its conception of 'face'. "One will know", a Byzantine might have reasoned, "that deception is intended by one's enemies, and that they will do their best to evade any possible charges that may lie to their account. But, at the same time, one does not say so openly." The delegation from the Crusaders and Venetians had committed the type of offence that Westerners were to be guilty of in their dealings with the East for centuries to come. The open affront of the one was met with the smooth words and concealed hatred of the other.

After this last formal encounter in the winter of 1203, there was no need for the relative positions of either parties to be any further established. The Byzantines, from court to courtyard, recognised the implacable nature of the people with whom they had to deal. The Crusaders for their part understood that they might expect no further cooperation from the other side. Villehardouin comments on "the treacherous nature of the Greeks", but seems surprised that the Byzantines had little faith in their dealings with him and the Crusaders.

Having delivered their ultimatum, the six ambassadors mounted their horses and spurred out from Blachernae. They were relieved to find themselves once more clear of those frowning walls and congratulated themselves on their escape. The ambassadors omitted to mention the fact that, if the Greeks had been half as capable of treachery as they were said to be, they themselves would never have been permitted to return to their camp. The Waring guard would have been delighted to cut them down, and the citizens who thronged their route on their way back to the walls were equally capable of seeing that they never left Blachernae alive. But the 'treacherous Greeks' let them go. Seeing that the Byzantines were already prepared and willing to undergo the rigours of a siege, it can hardly have been fear that caused them to treat the delegation in an honourable manner.

"Open war now began, each side doing its best to inflict damage upon the other, both by land and sea." It was during these months while the army shivered and suffered in its camp —"a measure of wine costing 14 sous, a hen 20 sous, and an egg 2 deniers"—that the influence of the Doge became paramount. Old though he was, and at the head of an alliance of various nationalities and conflicting interests, Enrico Dandolo managed to impose his will upon both fleet and army.

Boniface of Montferrat, although technically the leader of the Crusaders, seems to have suffered something of an eclipse. Whatever the cause—perhaps the fact that he had lost his influence over young Alexius—Boniface never again commanded so important a place in the expedition. It was the Doge, who thirty years before had lost his eyesight in Constantinople, who now directed his ambition—and perhaps his desire for revenge —to secure its capture. "It was always the Venetians who held us on our course and directed our aims. This was partly due to their determination to ensure that the money owing was paid,

but to some extent also to their ambition to secure for themselves the dominion of the sea . . ."*

On the night of January 1st, 1204, the Byzantines made their
first major attempt to destroy the Crusading army—or rather,
the fleet upon which its security depended. Having waited for
some days for a favourable southerly wind, they unleased an
attack by fireships on the Venetian galleys. One may possibly
trace the hand of Murtzuphlus in this bold attempt to annihilate
the enemy fleet. It is certain that neither Isaac nor Alexius
would have had the spirit, nor the necessary desire, to see their
Venetian friends destroyed.

Seventeen large vessels had been secretly filled with dry wood
and shavings, pitch and other inflammable materials. Their
square-sails were hoisted and they were directed across the
Horn towards the galleys and merchantmen lying at anchor on
the northern side. As always in a night engagement involving
fireships, everything depended upon the alertness and the
ability of those who were attacked. The Venetians (unlike the
Spaniards when similarly harassed by Drake in Calais some five
and a half centuries later), were neither dispirited nor demoralised. When the terrifying 'Hell-burners' came crackling down
towards their vessels they did not panic, even though "the
flames from them rose so high that the whole sea seemed to be
on fire".

Running down to the shore, the Venetians manned their
rowing-boats and swarmed aboard their galleys. While some
of them stood by with bearing-off spars to fend the blazing hulks
away from their ships, others went out in rowing-boats and
cast grappling-irons over the bulwarks of the fireships. Once
they had the ships firmly secured, they towed them away from
their galleys, out of the Golden Horn and into the swift-running
straits. One by one the fireships were grasped by the south-
flowing stream, and whirled away past the walls of Constantinople and into the Sea of Marmora.

Meanwhile the Byzantine forces manned the walls facing
across the Horn and other Greeks came out in small boats to
try and prevent the Venetian rescue operations. "Thousands
of the Greeks had come down to the water's edge and the noise

they made was enough to shake the earth itself. They opened fire on our men who were fighting against the fireships and wounded many of them." The Crusaders also heard the call to arms and came pouring out into the open plain opposite the walls of Blachernae. They half-expected to find the whole Greek army moving up to attack them.

It would indeed have been a good moment for a concentrated attack: for the army to have stormed the Crusaders' camp, while the Venetians were occupied aboard the galleys. The Byzantines missed their opportunity. Perhaps they had counted too much on the success of their fire-raid, calculating that if they destroyed the fleet there would never be any need to engage the Crusaders in an open battle. Certainly there can be no doubt that it was the skill and ability of the Venetians which saved the day. "And I, Geoffrey de Villehardouin who was an eyewitness of this affair, declare that never in history did any seamen act more gallantly than did the Venetians that night ... For if our fleet had been destroyed, we should have been unable to escape, either by land or by sea, and we should undoubtedly have been ruined."

This well-deserved tribute is followed by a remark so ingenuous that one wonders how even a simple-minded soldier could have written it without embarrassment: "Such was the way [the night attack] in which the Emperor Alexius acted as a return for all the services that we had done for him."

The failure of the fireships (only one Pisan merchantman was destroyed) marked the beginning of the end for Alexius. "This baby," as Murtzuphlus called him, had always been despised as the Crusaders' puppet. Had the attack succeeded and had the Crusaders been forced to capitulate, there can still be no doubt that Alexius was doomed. Even if the Venetians and Crusaders had been defeated, he would inevitably have been dethroned. The failure of the night attack merely served to stiffen the determination of the Byzantines to have done with this pinchbeck emperor. The party which cried for more action, and for no truckling to the enemy, was now seen to represent the true will of the people. The shout went up "Away with Alexius and his father! Away with all the Angeli family!

They have never done anything but bring disaster on the city."

On January 25th the confusion and anarchy reached such a peak that the court officials, nobles and clergy came to the unanimous decision that some action must be taken to restore order. The reins of power, which in any case had hardly ever been within the hands of Alexius, must be handed to a real emperor. A man must be found who was capable of exercising some firm control. "A great crowd gathered together in Santa Sophia, the whole senate and the high dignitaries of the Church. But when we had collected their votes," Nicetas tells us, "no conclusion could be reached as to who should be made Emperor if Alexius was deposed . . ."

The wrangling between one party and another went on for three days. The names of many members of the nobility were proposed, all of them for one reason or another being rejected. Murtzuphlus seems to have made no attempt to press his claims, He was preparing to take the power into his own hands. Finally, on the third day, a compromise was reached between the rival factions. A young nobleman, Nicholas Canobus, was elected emperor much against his will. This obscure figure who emerges for a brief moment on to the stage of history was wise in trying to repudiate so doubtful an honour. Only an ambitious, bold and resolute man would have been willing to be Emperor of Constantinople at such a moment.

Alexius was well aware of the meetings that were daily taking place in Santa Sophia, and sought his own safety by despatching a message to Boniface of Montferrat. He implored Boniface to come to his rescue and send troops to the palace to maintain him on the throne. This was the moment for which Murtzuphlus had been waiting. While the bulk of the court and all the officials were busy in Santa Sophia concluding the election of Nicholas Canobus, and while Alexius was waiting in fear to see whether the Crusaders would come to his rescue, Murtzuphlus struck.

Knowing that of all the troops in Constantinople only the Warings would be faithful to the death in defence of the Emperor, Murtzuphlus decided that before anything else he must make sure the imperial bodyguard had been withdrawn from their post. As *Protovestiarius* he had easy access to the imperial quarters, and as a confidant of Alexius the bodyguard assumed that he had the Emperor's interests at heart. Accordingly, Murtzuphlus entered the palace and told the Warings that a mob was on its way to dethrone and kill the Emperor. It was their duty, he said, to take up their stations outside and prevent the mob entering. The guards withdrew at the double. Murtzuphlus made his way to the Emperor and told him the same story, adding that he had come to help him escape. In his fear, Alexius forgot that the only people upon whose fidelity he could rely were the Warings.

Muffling himself in a cloak so as not to be recognised, he stole out of the palace along with his 'saviour'. Murtzuphlus conducted him to a meeting-place that had been arranged with the other conspirators. Once there, Alexius, protégé of Philip of Swabia and Emperor of Constantinople, was hurled to the ground and stripped of his insignia. He had been a pawn in the game from the very beginning and now, loaded with chains, he was 'removed from the board' and despatched to a dungeon. Murtzuphlus assumed the embroidered, pearl-studded, scarlet buskins and was hailed Emperor by his followers. So sudden and dramatic a *coup d'état* left the other nobles and ecclesiastics (who were even then electing Canobus Emperor) completely dumbfounded. Nicholas Canobus, reluctant recipient of an office he had never sought, was immediately abandoned. He passed out of the limelight into which he had been so unwillingly forced and retired into private life—almost certainly with some relief.

Murtzuphlus had acquired the throne by cunning and *force majeure*. But now that he had seized power, he was (by the peculiar nature of the Byzantine constitution) immediately accepted by the people as their rightful sovereign. Although, so long as he ruled, an emperor was supreme and not subject to human law, the moment that his office had been assumed by another it was an accepted fact that "Allegiance was automatically transferred. '*Le roi est mort*; *vive le roi*' was never truer than in the Byzantine world, even though the former occupant of the throne might have been most foully disposed of by his successor".*

Power belongs to him who holds it. Murtzuphlus was crowned in Santa Sophia with all the formality of Byzantine tradition. The Patriarch anointed him with the consecrated oil. The people acclaimed him as Emperor, 'King in Christ', and vice-regent of God on earth.

In the meantime the old co-Emperor, Isaac, had died. "He was overcome," according to Villehardouin, "by grief and illness brought on at the news of his son's arrest." De Clari says that he was strangled. Nicetas who, as a member of the court, was in a better position to know the true facts, agrees with Villehardouin that he died of old age and grief. Now if Nicetas could have found any further charges to lay at Murtzuphlus's door he would certainly have done so, for the office of Great Logothete (Lord Chancellor and Minister for Foreign Affairs), which Nicetas had held under Alexius, was now taken away from him.

Murtzuphlus was determined not to have any members of the former régime in position of power. All the historians are agreed about one aspect of this *coup d'état*—the fate of the unfortunate young Alexius. ". . . In the sixth month and eighth day of his reign he was strangled on the orders of Murtzuphlus." The new Emperor had no intention of making the same mistake that his predecessor had done. He was not going to leave a potential source of rebellion alive in the imperial dungeons. There could no longer be any possible argument for the Doge and the Crusaders that they were bent on restoring the legitimate ruler of Constantinople. Any further action that they took would have to be made openly—and on their own account.

II

THE CITY IN SPRING

THE news that Murtzuphlus had seized power, and that their protégé Alexius was imprisoned, caused consternation among the Venetians and Crusaders. With the removal of Alexius from the throne, any chance of his debts being paid had vanished. No one in Constantinople had any obligation for these. It was not as if he had been the chosen emperor of his people, for even Villehardouin could hardly convince himself that Alexius had been anything more than a puppet in the hands of Boniface and the Doge. During all these months the conspirators had at least been able to produce as excuse for the invasion of Byzantine territory that they were determined to restore the rightful emperor. Once they had restored him, there had been good reason for them all to remain outside Constantinople until such time as Alexius had discharged his debts. Now that he was dethroned and imprisoned (for they did not yet know that he was dead) it was quite clear that they could only recoup their losses by capturing the city.

Enrico Dandolo was never in his life "one of those sorry souls who", as Dante wrote, "live without either infamy or renown, displeasing both to God and his enemies". He was a man whom the great Florentine would have recognised—active, ambitious and prepared to die in battle rather than sink into an obscure and peaceful old age. He held the Crusaders in the palm of his hand, and he knew now (as they would learn shortly) that the only solution to their problems was to seize Constantinople and elect their own emperor.

Murtzuphlus, meanwhile, showed that the energy and audacity which had brought him to the throne were now at the service of the city.* He was a harsh and difficult man, never popular, and yet he managed to command an almost unwilling respect from the citizens of Constantinople during those dark days. Had he managed to achieve the throne at an earlier date —before the accession of Alexius and his father Isaac—it is quite possible that the Crusaders and the Venetians would have failed utterly in their object. He arrived too late to prevent the final catastrophe and yet, even at this moment in the history of the city and the Empire, he showed something of that spirit which had kept the barbarians at bay for so many centuries.

"The barons said that they would never abandon the siege until they had taken their revenge and captured the city a second time—and had complete payment of Alexius's debts to them. When Murtzuphlus heard their intention he gave orders for the walls and towers to be manned, and to be further strengthened . . ." He would not permit any of the citizens to shirk their obligations, levying further taxes on the rich (although, unlike those of young Alexius, these were not to pay the enemy but to defeat him), and compelling everyone to work night and day on the fortifications. The weak points of the defences, the harbour walls facing the Golden Horn which the Venetians had managed to storm, were the first major consideration. Gangs of labourers were set to work raising the level of the battlements, so that the Venetian drawbridges would no longer be able to reach the top of the walls. Above the seaward towers themselves Murtzuphlus had two- to three-storied wooden stages erected, so that the archers and crossbowmen would have additional advantage over any Venetian attempts to run up scaling ladders from the bows of their galleys.

Everywhere—and for the first time since the Crusading fleet had been seen off the walls of the city in June the previous year —a sense of purpose and urgency existed. Murtzuphlus was a man of action. He did not spare himself but was to be found during the course of a day, now at the head of the cavalry as they cut off parties of Crusaders foraging for fuel and food in the nearby country, and now among the workmen on the walls of the city. His conduct and his spirit won the grudging respect of his people. For the first time for many years they felt that they had a man of character to lead them. But if the ordinary citizens admired and followed him, the nobility (and Nicetas the historian was very typical of them) disliked him intensely. They felt the pinching pressure of his tax-collectors and resented it. Grown soft under the rule of indulgent and corrupt emperors, they objected strongly to the curtailment of their privileges and to the constant reminder that they too must live under siege conditions.

Murtzuphlus had indeed taken on an almost impossible task. The treasury was exhausted; a large and important part of the city lay in ruins; and almost the last of their shipping had been lost in the ill-fated fireship raid. Furthermore, the army was disorganised, and largely unpaid. It was little wonder that Murtzuphlus had no time to indulge the privileged nobles, and that they for their part grew to hate the sight of him. His attitude towards them was tyrannical but, under the circumstances, realistic. As Nicetas tells us, "They feared his voice like that of death."

The party which was all for peace at any price—so long as their own comfort could be maintained—wanted to see Boniface of Montferrat made emperor. Whether they were in fact faint-hearts or realists, these members of the rich and merchant classes had long ago given up any hope of defeating the Venetians and Crusaders. They longed for normal conditions to return, and they thought that the best way of securing this would be to enthrone the man who had been the protector of young Alexius, and who was the leader of the Crusaders.

This group contrived to hamper Murtzuphlus in every way they could, and to prepare for the day when they could unseat him and hand over the throne to Boniface. But if Murtzuphlus did not command the following of the wealthy, he had managed to win the Waring guard to his side. Infuriated at first by the discovery of how he had tricked them in order to seize the Emperor Alexius, they had now given him their entire confidence. For one thing, they respected the fact that this emperor was a man of action, and for another they now learned how Alexius had been preparing to call in the Normans to protect him at the moment that Murtzuphlus had struck. One authority also stated categorically that the failure of the fireship raid was due to the fact that the Emperor Alexius had secretly warned the enemy in advance.* When the Warings heard of this piece of treachery, they gladly espoused the cause of Murtzuphlus, an emperor who was clearly determined to do all that he could to keep the Franks and Normans out of the city.

In the early spring of that year, as the winter receded and far north across the Black Sea the snows withdrew, the city began to quicken with a renewed life. The small craft were creeping up from the islands of the Aegean, from the coastal villages of Thrace and from the Morea. Spring is slower to reach Constantinople than the Peloponnese, the mainland of Greece or the islands. Although few merchants put to sea in Greek waters until the 'prodoms'—those forerunners of the northern winds of midsummer—began to blow, yet there were always some who were prepared to risk their craft and dodge up the coast in order to arrive early at the city. Quite soon the traders would be coming down from the Black Sea, from the ports of Heraclea, Amastris, Sinope and Trebizond. The overland route from the north would reopen and the merchants from Mesembria and Varna, from Wallachia beyond the Danube and from Russia itself would start to arrive. Amber would come from the distant Baltic, furs and skins from Petchinak and Wallach trappers, and soon by the overland Asian route spices, perfumes, ivory and raw silk would filter through from India and China. Despite the Seljuk Turks lying athwart the roads to Persia and Syria, precious stones, cotton and sugar still made their way to the ancient capital from the Levant.

The city was not only a consumer but an exporter of many manufactured goods—woven silks, carved ivories, enamelled jewellery, ceramic wares and metal goods of all kinds. As an important centre of the re-export trade Constantinople, even at this period in its history, was an invaluable link between the cultures and the mercantile centres of Asia and Europe. Turkish merchants as well as other Moslems were frequent visitors (as witness the 'Saracen' mosque that had caused the recent riot and led to the disastrous fire). One chronicler of the Crusades went so far as to say that: "It would have been right to have razed the city to the ground, for it was polluted by mosques which its treacherous emperor had allowed to be built in order to strengthen his trade with the Turks".

Even in the spring of 1204 Constantinople was the most cosmopolitan city in the world. The Spanish Jew, Benjamin of Tudela, who visited the city forty-one years before the Fourth Crusade, commented on the merchants who "came from all corners of the earth, from Egypt and Babylon, Mesopotamia and Palestine, Hungary, Spain and Russia". Despite the terrible losses sustained in the fire, and despite the fact that the city was invested by a Crusading army and fleet, it was still supreme. The New Rome, dignified by its great Christian churches and decorated with the works of art that had been salvaged from the wreck of the ancient world, was incomparably splendid. As an envoy from Khiev once wrote: "God dwells there among men. We cannot forget that beauty."

The main artery of the city was the Triumphal Way which started in the south at the Golden Gate, the imposing arch through which the emperors returned after expeditions in the field. The great thoroughfare ran almost parallel with the Marmora walls, passing through the Forum of Arcadius and the Forum of the Bull (beneath which flowed the river Lycus to enter the sea in the harbour of Eleutherius). Mesé Street joined it just north of this point, and from here the Triumphal Way swept eastwards through the great Forum of Theodosius and the Forum of Constantine to terminate by the Hippodrome. Never perhaps in the history of the world was there a city so graced with statues, with monuments and obelisks: statues from the Roman Empire, from classical Greece and from Egypt and the East; and monuments of victors and to triumphs spanning more than a thousand years of history.

In the imperial Hippodrome, which was capable of holding 60,000 spectators, the sunlight glanced along the banked rows of white marble seats. Nine hundred feet long and over four hundred feet wide, the Hippodrome held among its other treasures the famous column of the Three Serpents. This was

the oldest and most awe-inspiring of all Constantinople's innumerable monuments. It dated from the Persian invasion of
Greece and had once supported the golden tripod found by the
Greeks among the Persian loot after the battle of Plataea.
Dedicated to Apollo, it had stood for centuries at Delphi, until
removed by Constantine to grace the imperial city, Here, too,
were the four colossal bronze horses (which now occupy the
centre of the gallery of St. Mark's in Venice). They had been
brought to Constantinople from Chios by the Emperor Theodosius in the fifth century. Near by was the huge column of
porphyry erected by Constantine to commemorate the founda-
tion of the city. It reputedly housed in its base that symbol of
empire, the sacred Palladium which Aeneas had taken from
Troy to Rome, and which Constantine had removed to his new
capital to show that the genius of Rome now resided on the
Bosphorus. An Egyptian obelisk, reminder that the Byzantine
Empire had once embraced all Egypt, the Near East and the
shores of North Africa, was decorated round its marble base
with scenes from the imperial games.

Everywhere the city shone with marble or gleamed with
bronzes. Through the immense aqueduct of Valens the water
flowed in from the countryside to supply the cisterns, the baths
and the fountains. Built in the fourth century, it had been
extensively restored and improved in the eighth when, as a
chronicler tells us: "Workmen were brought from many places
to rebuild it—a thousand from Asia and Pontus, and two
hundred whitewashers and five hundred brick-makers from
Greece, and a thousand day-labourers from Thrace."

All over the city, light gleamed and sparkled from acres of
lake-like reservoirs.* By the diversion of streams and rivers, by
its open and its underground reservoirs, the city had achieved
a water-supply that was to be unequalled in Europe until the
Industrial Revolution. Nowhere before, except perhaps in
ancient Rome, had the citizens of any capital enjoyed so
abundant a water-supply, nor—those other amenities of the
modern age—such efficient sanitation and drainage. To the
Crusaders, whose own experience of cities was limited to the
squalor of medieval townships (often perched somewhat

uneasily on the remains of great Roman buildings), Constantinople was always a revelation.

Beyond the Hippodrome, the rambling Sacred Palace of the Emperors descended in buildings, courts, galleries and terraced gardens to the edge of the Marmora. Here the wall swept round from the delightful small church of SS. Sergius and Bacchus to take in the whole area of the Acropolis. At the easternmost corner of what is now Seraglio Point, the gate of Saint Barbara gave on to the sea. Not far from here an inscription on the curtain wall challenged the forces of man and nature:

> *Possessing Thee, O Christ, a wall unbreakable,*
> *Theophilus the King and pious emperor*
> *Has raised this wall upon a new foundation.*
> *O King of All Things, guard it under thy protection*
> *And show it till the end of time unshakeable*
> *And indestructible . . ."**

Even in this hard spring, with a hostile army encamped outside the walls and the whole of the Golden Horn occupied by an enemy fleet, life still flowed through the streets and industry carried on. The sound of the artisans' hammers rang out from the quarter of the coppersmiths and metal-workers. The tanners, with an unhappy disregard for the sensibilities of passers-by, emptied their evil-smelling vats into the street drains in the quarter of the tanners and leather workers. Everything was extreme. There was no 'Golden mean' for, although the New Rome was a Greek city, it was a far remove from the Periclean world. Poverty and wealth were incongruously juxtaposed. A huge palace enriched with marble columns and mosaics sprang suddenly out of a huddle of ramshackle wooden dwellings. A fountain of marble sparkled in the centre of a dusty square where horse droppings, the stench of burning hair and the clang of hammer on anvil marked the quarter of the blacksmiths and ironworkers. In the area inhabited by jewellers and enamellers silence reigned, broken only by the tap-tap of small gnome-like hammers or the buzzing of the lapidary's drill.

There were many things, particularly in the poorer quarters of the city, that would remind the Crusaders of their own towns,

yet everything in Constantinople was on so vast a scale that
even the most cynical traveller could not repress a sigh of
admiration. As Benjamin of Tudela remarked—and he had
many criticisms to make of the city—"Strongholds are filled
with garments of silk, purple and gold. There is nothing in the
whole world to be found to equal these store-houses and this
wealth. The Greek inhabitants are very rich in gold and
precious stones, and they go clothed in garments of silk with
gold embroidery, and they ride horses, and look like princes.
Indeed, the land is very rich in all cloth stuffs, and in bread,
meat and wine. Wealth like that of Constantinople is not to be
found in the whole world."*

As in most hot countries, the houses of the middle class and
of the rich presented blank faces to the streets and sidewalks.
Their life was turned inwards, centred around the courtyards
where fountains played into fish tanks, and where statuary
gleamed under marble walks shadowed by vines. Occasionally
a bow-window would project from the second floor of such a
house and the passer-by could make out the shadowy forms of
the ladies as they chattered and sewed, or used the street as
their theatre. Wood smoke scented the air, for it was still cold
in March, and in the streets charcoal braziers glowed, where
chickens and ribbon-like spirals of gut stuffed with forcemeat
(forerunner of the modern sausage) turned on spits. There were
vegetable and fruit gardens within the city walls, and the
barrows of pedlars were piled high with their produce, as well
as with caviare, imported dates, sugar, cinnamon and ginger.
Despite the siege, the fishing-boats were still working out of the
harbours of Boucoleon, Julian, Contoscalion and Eleutherius
on the Marmora. The cold waters of the Bosphorus yielded an
immense quantity and variety of fish. Meat was something of a
luxury, but bread, vegetables, olives and olive oil produced a
diet that was simple but healthy.

Despite the events of the past nine months the streets presented a scene of extraordinary liveliness and colour. The con-
trasting dress of the various classes made for variety—the workmen in their short tunics and sandals, the rich in longer tunics
of bright colours with soft leather boots, and the women in their

ankle-length robes, with their head-dresses of silk. Men and
women alike were bedecked with jewellery (an effeminate
custom, the Crusaders thought). Heavy gold and silver brace-
lets gleamed on the men's wrists and forearms, while the women
wore elaborate filigree necklaces—gold and silver set with
precious stones and enlivened by enamels. Delicate pendant
ear-rings danced as they walked.

The magnificent traditions of the classical Greek and Roman
jewellers had been preserved in Constantinople, and had been
married to the complex design and colourful palette of the
east. In the palace the official costumes were as elaborate and
ornate as the combined experience of the silk-makers and the
court-jewellers could make them. Gloves and slippers were
sewn with pearls, while the dalmatic (a long, wide-sleeved
garment worn over a silk tunic) was decorated with embroidery.
Over and above this came the bejewelled and embroidered
pallium, which hung down at the back to form a train that was
looped and carried over the left arm. It was little wonder that
the knights in their coarse but practical chain-mail felt something like contempt, even if mingled with uneasy admiration,
for these flower-like people.

Decayed though the city was since the days of its great
splendours, weakened by corrupt administration and by the
losses sustained throughout its territories during the past
century, it had an autumnal magnificence about it in these last
days. The example set by Murtzuphlus infused a new spirit
into the citizens. Even though it was too little and too late, a
memory of their former pride seemed to return to the Byzantines. It still seemed possible that the God-guarded walls would
save them. They could not believe that the relics of the Holy
Cross, and of all the martyrs and saints that had protected them
so often in the past, would not once again intervene.

Hope returns with the spring. Soon the chanting priests
would be telling them that Christ had risen once again, that
He had indeed risen, and that in this Easter of the year 1204
He had saved and secured his chosen city from the enemy. Was
it not Christ Himself who had ordained the circuit of the walls?
When the Emperor Constantine, spear in hand, was tracing out

the lines that his new capital was to follow, he was asked by one of his courtiers how much farther he intended to go. The Emperor had replied: "Until He tarries who now goes before me."

Christ, who had ordained the shape that the city was to take, had saved it from all its enemies for nearly nine centuries of constant threat, attack and siege. It was not to be believed that this time the Queen of Cities would be forced to her knees. And yet there were always pessimists. "In the damp, melancholy climate of the Bosphorus the natural gaiety of the Greeks was dimmed. Even in the great days of the Empire men had whispered that it would not last for ever. It was well known that on stones throughout the city and in the books written by the sages of the past the list of emperors was written, and it was drawing to an end."*

It is true that, as the local saying has it, "There are two climates in Constantinople: that of the north wind, and that of the south wind". Neither are invigorating, for even the north wind is not without humidity, while the south wind is like all south winds in the Mediterranean area—debilitating and relaxing. The adjective 'Byzantine', when used in its pejorative senses as indicative of anything that is unnecessarily double-faced and tortuous, might certainly be applied to the climate. Neither the torrid dry heat of summer Athens nor its equally harsh but invigorating winter was known in distant Constantinople.

Murtzuphlus was trying to combat a languor that was bred in the bone, and which had only been accentuated by the events of the past century. If he still managed to carry with him many of the working people as well as the Waring Guard, he could not light a patriotic fire in the hearts of the nobles, or the court officials. Meanwhile the eunuchs, whose influence was considerable in the treasury, the Civil Service and other important offices of State, pursued their caponised course—careless of everything save their own comfort.

It is a true statement that "Nature, indeed, cannot relieve men of their duty to be wise and brave, but, in the marvellous configuration of land and sea about Constantinople, nature has done her utmost to enable human skill and courage to establish there the splendid and stable throne of a great empire."* In that March of 1204 the Crusaders and Venetians were still confronted with the most formidable walled city in the world. They themselves were between the devil and the deep. If they failed to take the city or were defeated, the only escape route for them from this hostile corner of northern Thrace was by sea. Yet if they failed to take the city, they had no means of paying the Venetians whose fleet was their only means of escape. While the Byzantines could afford the psychological luxury of relaxing, as it were, on the laurelled memory of their past triumphs, the Crusaders were driven by sheer necessity. Whatever Murtzuphlus might achieve by his example and efforts among his own people, he had nothing to equal the iron goad that was wielded by Dandolo over the Crusaders.

12

PREPARATIONS FOR ATTACK

THE news that now reached the Crusaders from the Holy Land and Syria was enough to daunt even the few who were still enthusiastic for their true mission. Their comrades who had proceeded independently had suffered nothing but disaster. A large proportion of the group which had sailed from Marseilles had reached Syria only to be decimated by disease. Others who had been engaged against the Turks were either dead or enslaved.

The original object of their expedition seemed far away, and less and less desirable. The Crusade that was to have landed in Egypt, captured Alexandria and cut the Moslem world in half, had already failed. The attractions of Constantinople were ever-present before their eyes, and in a number of engagements round and about the city they had quickly discovered their superiority over the Byzantine troops.

From the moment that the death of Alexius had been confirmed, the influence of Boniface of Montferrat had been on the wane. Alexius had been his protégé, and the scheme which he and Philip of Swabia had hatched had no meaning once Alexius was dead. Any idea of uniting the western and eastern empires was at an end. All that Boniface could now hope for was that the army should capture Constantinople and proclaim him emperor. He had his well-wishers inside the city, and it would be no mean thing to be the first Latin emperor of the Byzantine world. At the same time he would be able to purge himself of guilt in the Pope's eyes if it was he who healed the schism between the churches and made a unity out of Christendom. But as far as Doge Dandolo was concerned, the usefulness of Boniface was almost at an end. Dandolo must preserve a superficial amity with him so as to ensure the support of the Crusaders, but he had other plans as to who should be ruler of Constantinople once the city had been taken.

Early in March the barons met in council. The proceedings were stormy and the leaders were far from united, but by now it was plain to all that they had no option but to fall in with the Venetian design. The news from the East had daunted the pro-Syria party, and even those most hostile to the idea of storming yet another Christian city were forced to recognise that there was no other way out for them. The stranglehold which Dandolo had gained on the Crusaders so many months ago had now become inexorable. Even the simplest-minded Crusaders could not ignore it. As for the majority of the army, dispirited, having long lost any interest in the real purpose of their voyage, they longed only for some recompense for the uneasy months of waiting and of existing on half-rations in foreign camps. Constantinople the Golden presented a vision of loot far beyond their expectations in Egypt or Syria. A formal agreement was now reached between all parties that they should undertake the siege.

They also laid it down that if they should be successful in taking the city, "all the plunder should be brought to one place and there fairly shared out among the troops." But the problem of how to achieve the necessary discipline over the troops to ensure this was never discussed. The parliament of barons and Venetians also came to the decision that the election of a new emperor should be decided by twelve delegates; six Crusaders and six Venetians. A corollary to this was that the Patriarch of the city should be a Venetian if a Crusader was elected emperor, and vice-versa.

"Whoever the new emperor might be, it was agreed that he should have one quarter of all the captured treasure in Constantinople, as well as the two imperial palaces of Boucoleon and Blachernae. The remaining three-quarters of the booty should be equally divided between Venetians and Crusaders." They also agreed, De Clari tells us, "to see that no woman was molested, that no members of the clergy were harmed, that convents and churches were not damaged, and that any man guilty of such things should be put to death. This they swore to on sacred relics." Having settled to their own satisfaction the division of the spoils and the fate of the imperial city, the fleet and the army began to prepare for the attack.

While the soldiers made ready the mangonels, catapults and other siege-engines, and the Venetians got their ships into battle-order, the leaders met to decide on the best plan of attack. In view of the fact that the army was not large enough to take on the Byzantines in a pitched battle, the Venetians' plan of a mass seaborne assault on the walls facing the Golden Horn was adopted. This had been the Doge's suggestion the previous year, but it had been rejected by the barons who had maintained that they and their men were only experienced in fighting on land, and that their special abilities would be wasted if they came as marines aboard the ships. But the Venetians' success against the sea-walls on the Golden Horn had demonstrated that here, at any rate, the city was vulnerable, and the Crusaders' own poor showing against the Warings during their landward attack on Blachernae had convinced them that they would do better to combine their forces. Their willingness to accede to the Venetian plan of attack points to the fact that it was Doge Dandolo who was now master-minding the whole expedition.

On Friday morning, April 9th, 1204, the great attack began. The Venetian galleys were ranged on the northern side of the Golden Horn ready to tow across the palanders containing the armoured knights, men-at-arms and the horses. The scaling bridges which had proved so successful before were hoisted up by tackles from the masts. The rock- and spear-hurling catapults in the bows of the transports were manned. The whole line of battle stretched nearly a mile and a half, from Blachernae to just beyond the district of Petrion in the city. Murtzuphlus, who had been watching the preparations throughout the preceding days, had set up his headquarters on the hill just behind Petrion. He thus had the whole of the threatened area under his immediate surveillance.

The area selected by the Doge and the Venetians for the

assault was the one where they had been so successful the previous summer. Although Murtzuphlus had strengthened the
wall and the towers at this point, the attackers felt confident
that once again they would be able to establish a foothold on
the ramparts. The fleet touched down on the muddy flatland
at the foot of the walls without much difficulty, and the Crusaders began hastily to disembark their siege-engines. At the
same time trained groups of sappers ran forward under cover
of 'tortoise-shells' (or hide-protected carts) to start undermining
the walls. As they brought up their battering-rams the air
above them resounded to the cries of battle, as armed men ran
up the covered gangways and grappled with the defenders on
the parapets. Having secured their bows to the shore, the
Venetians threw out stern anchors to keep their ships pointed
like daggers at the defences of Constantinople. Lying farther off
at anchor, the heavier transports that had been converted into
floating catapult-platforms kept up a steady fire upon the
defenders.

But many things had changed since the previous Venetian
attack. Murtzuphlus had been astute in having the height of
the walls raised and in erecting subsidiary wooden towers
above the stone battlements. Soon the Byzantine catapults
were finding their targets among the armada anchored within
easy range of the walls. The siege-engines that the Crusaders
had dragged on to the foreshore were the first to suffer, as huge
rocks boomed down to crush them and the men serving them.
The sappers under their flimsy protections were unable to stay
at the foot of the walls and were forced to retreat. Soon even
the galleys and merchant ships began to come under fire, as the
Byzantines got their range and turned their catapults upon the
immobile targets.

"And soon they were beginning to break to pieces the siege-
engines on the shore, so that no one dare man them. The
Venetians for their part could not get close enough to the walls
or the towers, because they had been made so much taller.
Neither section of our forces was having any success so, seeing
that the attack was failing, they were reluctantly forced to
withdraw." It was three o'clock in the afternoon when Murt-

zuphlus and his staff saw that the first assault was over. Men were running back down the foreshore to the ships, the galleys were getting up their anchors, and the whole line of invasion craft was beginning to make its way back across the Horn. Only a few of the heavier merchantmen, armed with catapults and mangonels, were staying put at anchor off the shore. The Greeks raised a cheer, and along all the battlemented walls facing the Golden Horn the cry was taken up as the defenders saw the hated enemy withdrawing. Once again in their long history the God-guarded walls had saved the people of the city.

That night the tense and grim-faced leaders of the army and the fleet met to consider their position. They had suffered severe losses, while the Byzantines had had hardly any casualties. Their frontal attack on the walls had been easily repulsed, and there were many who now urged the commanders to reconsider their plan of attack. "The walls here are now too strong," they said. "Let us move the ships down to the seaward mouth of the Horn. It is plain that the defences are less formidable there, for the Greeks have not had time to repair them."

It was true that Murtzuphlus and his commanders had not paid much attention to the walls near Acropolis Point, but they had good reason not to be concerned about them. The Venetians, with their knowledge of the sea, were quick to point out why an attack on Constantinople at the mouth of the Horn was doomed to fail.

"The current near the mouth runs so fast," they said, "that it would be almost impossible to hold our ships in order against the shore. If we should beach our ships there they would be caught by the current and the anchors could not hold them. The next thing that would happen is that the ships would break loose and be carried willy-nilly down the Bosphorus."

Their superior knowledge of seamanship carried conviction. The Lombard, French and Belgian knights might be adept on horseback, but they were ignorant of the sea and its ways, and they were willing to accept the words of the premier sea-going nation in Europe. Even so, as Villehardouin remarks, "there were some who would have been only too happy if the current could indeed have carried them down the straits. They no longer cared where they went—only so long as it took them away from this country."

In the end it was decided to spend the next two days, Saturday and Sunday, repairing the damage to the ships, the landing equipment, and the siege-engines, and to renew the attack on Monday at exactly the same place. During the day's fighting the attackers had noticed that when one ship attacked a tower with its assault-ramp it had been unsuccessful because there were enough men on the tower to repel the boarders. They decided therefore to lash the ships together two abreast, so that they would be able to disgorge double the number of men at the same time. While the soldiers rested over the weekend, the sailors worked, binding the assault galleys into pairs and ensuring that the gangways were well secured so that both ships could discharge their men simultaneously.

The clergy, meanwhile, were not slow to notice that the troops needed some boost to their morale. They told them that "They judged this struggle to be an honourable one. The people of Constantinople were no more than heretics for they did not accept the rule of Rome. For this reason it was the soldiers' duty to give battle. Far from being a sin, it was on the contrary a pious act." Villehardouin records that the priests told the troops, "The battle is lawful and just. If you show the right spirit in conquering this land and putting it in obedience to Rome, all those of you who die will certainly have the Pope's absolution for your sins . . ."

The knowledge that, far from suffering excommunication as had been their fate after the capture of Zara, they would go blameless to Heaven if they fell in battle, had an immense effect upon the morale of the Crusaders. In the days when men believed that if they died unabsolved they were doomed to hell, the knowledge that they were promised Paradise in the afterlife gave them an almost Berserker eagerness for the fray. As a mild reminder that not even heaven can be attained without some element of self-sacrifice, the clergy ordered them "to chase all the loose women out of the camp. So accordingly they put them all in a boat and sent them on their way"—presumably not too far away.

While the Crusaders were attending Mass and receiving absolution, the Byzantines settled down to await the next attack. They were in a far greater mood of confidence than at any time since the invaders had first arrived off their shores the previous summer. They had seen the dreaded Venetian fleet retire damaged, and the bodies of many Crusaders still lay unburied and unblessed on the mud foreshore below their ramparts and towers. The Orthodox priests had invoked the blessings of the Saints, and many a citizen had visited one of the innumerable churches of Constantinople to take comfort from the wonder-working relics that lay enshrouded in their ikons and bejewelled reliquaries. Superstition was not a prerogative of either side. Both believed confidently in the righteousness of their cause and in the Christian God who would see the triumph of their arms.

There was no wind at dawn on Monday, April 12th. Silently the sailors and soldiers took up their positions aboard the galleys, landing-craft and merchantmen. On the walls facing them the Byzantine sentries paced up and down, feeling the morning damp strike up at them from the quiet waters. Clouds were banking up over the land to the north of Galata. In the Emperor Murtzuphlus's camp near the monastery of Pantepoptis at Petrion messengers arrived to say that the looked-for activity among the enemy had started. Lights began to twinkle from the scarlet imperial tent and soon the Emperor himself was afoot. Soldiers were taking up their stations along the turreted battlements facing the Horn. Bugles sounded, their thin brazen cries mingling with the cockcrows of dawn. The night mist began to lift off the city, peeling away from the reservoirs and aqueducts, vegetable and fruit gardens, and the slumbering courtyards of the rich. Fishing-boats were putting out into the Marmora from the small harbours and from the beaches below the Asia-facing walls.

Southward by the Golden Gate carts were rumbling in from the countryside, and the sails of fishing-boats and small merchantmen flickered far out in the Marmora as their crews hoisted canvas to catch whatever wind dawn might bring. The sun came up over Asia and lit the long line of the sea-walls. The city stood poised and waiting, balanced on the knife-edge between night and day. Now the boom of the time-keepers' gongs was heard and the shrill of overseers' whistles. The water on the far side of the Golden Horn began to stir into life, and the great assault was launched.

13

INTO THE BREACH

THE Byzantines awaited the approach of the attacking fleet with confidence. As the galleys and transports neared the shore they kept up a steady fire, cheering whenever a missile crashed aboard one of the enemy ships, or hurled the broad sweeps of the galley's oars asunder. But there was no turning back for the invaders.

"The noise was so great," Villehardouin wrote, "that it seemed as if the whole earth was disintegrating." Greek fire spouted from the ramparts, hissing and splattering among the men on the foreshore. The Crusaders, who had learned the use of Greek fire and other combustibles during their eastern campaigns, retorted in kind; discharging liquid fire from tubes high up in the assault-ramps of the ships. "But the fire had no effect on the wooden towers," De Clari remarks, "for they were all sheathed in skins." The Byzantine stone-throwing catapults had little more effect on the ships which were breaching opposite the towers, for the Venetians had built sturdy coverings of wood over the foredecks and the oar-benches. These had been covered with dense layers of brushwood and vine-branches to break the force of rocks and other projectiles.

Murtzuphlus meanwhile was watching the engagement from the hill of Petrion. The church bells clamoured out a warning to the citizens that the city was being attacked, trumpets sounded and messengers scurried back and forth from the Emperor's side. As he watched the tide of battle, he ordered reinforcements to be moved to a threatened area, or withdrew men from a section of wall where it was clear that no attack might be expected. It looked as if the events of the previous day were to be repeated. The Byzantines seemed to be causing more casualties in the ships and the beach parties than the latter were able to inflict upon them. Then the clouds which had been looming up over the Black Sea for the past twenty-four hours sent on their advance messenger—the wind. "And it pleased God, "as Villehardouin piously wrote, "that a wind called Boreas should blow and it was this which drove the ships hard on to the shore . . ."

Not only did the wind push the ships farther up the foreshore than the oarsmen could ever have driven them but it also prevented any chance of retreat. There was no option for the invaders now; they were as irrevocably committed as if they had burned their boats behind them. The crisping waves that followed them up the beach, and that ground the bows of their ships farther and farther into the soil of Byzantium were like sword-thrusts driving the soldiers and the sappers ever forward against the frowning walls.

As is often the case in that part of the world, the northerly wind grew stronger as the sun climbed towards its zenith. The short breaking seas running down across the half-mile of open water began to lift and bounce the ships forward over the sand, mud and pebbles of the foreshore. The *Pilgrim* and the *Paradise*, two ships which had been bound together to make an assault-platform, were gradually lifted forward until their landing-ramp came level with one of the towers. A Venetian managed to jump over from the swaying bridges and forced his way into the top storey of the tower. He was immediately hacked to pieces by a group of Warings who were guarding this topmost point. At this moment, a sudden gust of wind drove the two vessels hard against the tower, so that the Venetian sailors were able to get grappling-irons on to its structure and lash the vessels securely to the wall. A French knight, André Durboise, bravely followed the lead of his Venetian predecessor and jumped into the tower. Within seconds he was followed by others, some leaping from the landing-ramp and others crawling up from the bows of the vessels and assaulting the lower stages of the defences. Robert de Clari pays a tribute to the benefits of armour: "The English and the Danes rushed at him [Durboise] and if he had not been wearing armour they would have cut him down . . ."

Now that the two ships were firmly secured to the tower by ropes and grappling-irons, the towers began to shake as the ships pounded up and down in the ever-increasing sea. The defenders feeling the tower tremble beneath them and equally unnerved by the impetuous inrush of the enemy, began to retreat stage by stage down to the solid wall beneath. While this tower was gradually being overwhelmed, yet another pair of ships jostled forward by the north wind came hard against a neighbouring tower. The same process was repeated.

On the foreshore near by, encouraged by the assault on these two towers, bands of soldiers began to work against one of the city gates with battering-rams and pickaxes. De Clari singles out for mention among the attackers his own brother, Aliaume de Clari. The latter was in clerical orders, but seems to have been a fire-eater for he had already distinguished himself in the attack the previous year on the tower at Galata. Despite the loads of burning pitch which the defenders discharged over the parapets upon Aliaume and his companions as they strove to break down the gate, the attackers managed to splinter a gap through the thick wooden planks that opposed them.

Aliaume, followed by his brother the historian, was among the first to burst through this hole into Constantinople. They were soon joined by some sixty men-at-arms and a number of armoured knights. "Once they were inside, the men above them on the walls and the others who were in this quarter of the city panicked and did not dare oppose them. The Greeks began to flee, and as they fled so more and more joined them. The Emperor Murtzuphlus, that traitor, who was near by— less than a stone's throw, in fact—ordered all the bells to be rung and the trumpets to sound."

All men who are engaged in battle tend to think that it is their own detachment which has, in fact, made the breach and opened the way for the rest of their companions. Whether it was the two de Claris does not really matter: the fact remains that, almost at the same time as the two towers were being overwhelmed, one of the small city gates that gave on to the sea was broken open and the attackers made an entry into Constantinople. A French knight Pierre de Bracheux, seeing the group around him hesitate as they found themselves within the city, rallied them: "Now, sirs, now is the moment of triumph! We shall soon win the day! Look, that's the Emperor himself who's heading our way. Let no one think of flying now, for this is the very moment when we must acquit ourselves like men!"

Murtzuphlus, however, did not bring his Waring bodyguard to the attack, but contented himself with summoning up reinforcements to the area where the invaders had secured their foothold in the city. It was a mistake. Before the reinforcements had arrived, the small force that was within the walls had managed to open another nearby gate—not a small postern this time, but one big enough to admit men on horseback. As soon as this became known, the transports raised their anchors and beached themselves near the spot. Very soon the men-at-arms were leading the horses ashore, the knights mounted and the armoured cavalry was storming into the city.

This was the very moment when a determined attack by Murtzuphlus and his troops could still have turned the day. They had the advantage of being on higher ground, and they had had several hours in which to prepare a plan of campaign should the enemy manage to break into the city at any point. Unfortunately the imperial cavalry were not of the same mettle as the mercenary Waring guard. Commanded by the aristocracy, many of whom were hostile to Murtzuphlus, they were as panic-stricken as were most of the native Byzantine troops. Being less well-armoured than the western knights, they were not prepared to rally to the Emperor's support, or to charge the invaders as they burst into the city. At the sight of the French and Normans streaming ashore from the transports and pouring in through the open gate on their warhorses, the Byzantine cavalry lost its nerve and fled.*

Murtzuphlus, who had done all he could to put heart into his troops, found himself abandoned in the face of the invaders. As the mounted knights began to stream up the hill towards him he retreated through the streets, followed by his foot soldiers and the faithful Waring guard. He made his way across the city towards the ancient imperial palace of Boucoleon —that complex of buildings running down to the Marmora. In that network of reception-chambers, chapels, artificers' quarters, playgrounds and gardens, it might still be possible to offer some resistance.

The Byzantine troops manning the walls facing the Golden Horn were aghast to see the Crusaders streaming into the city beneath them. The assault from the galleys and from the transports redoubled as the Venetians realised that the Crusaders had made a breach in the walls and were safely established. Caught between the attacking enemy by sea and the enemy who were now at their back, the defenders began to desert their posts on the walls and retreat into the city. The knights and men-at-arms who had stormed the deserted hill of Petrion overran the headquarters of the Emperor. They swept through the brocaded tents, looting and pillaging as they went.

From here they looked down upon the city as it lay to the south of them, tranquil in the afternoon sun. There was nothing to show from the smoking chimneys and the placid reservoirs and orchards that for the first time in history an invader was established within the sacred walls.

"Three miles wide and three miles long was the city within its walls," writes Robert de Clari, "and the circumference of its walls was so great that a man could easily get lost within it . . . everyone was advised to stay where they were and not to press on into the interior. For there was always the possibility that men might be killed by having stones hurled down on them from the roofs, while many of the streets were so narrow that a man would be at the mercy of the inhabitants".

The decision was taken to hold the Petrion area and to set up their own headquarters on the hill. The walls and the city immediately behind them were already held by their own troops, so there was no danger of being attacked from the rear. In these circumstances it was only sensible to rest for the night, while further troops, armaments and ammunition were landed from the transports. They settled down and made themselves ready to give battle the following morning.

But in the meantime the occupied area of the city had been subject to fire and sword. Even Villehardouin admits that "so many Greeks were killed that it was impossible to count them. They and their animals, their horses and their mules were cut down, and all their possessions seized. Hundreds of the inhabitants fled towards the Blachernae gates, but by this time our men had grown tired of fighting and slaughtering, for it was past six in the evening. So they assembled in one of the great squares of Constantinople and, having realised that it would take them at least a month to conquer the whole city, they decided to rest there for the night . . ."

While the Marquis of Montferrat encamped south of Petrion nearest to the unconquered area of Constantinople, Count Baldwin of Flanders occupied the imperial tents so recently deserted by Murtzuphlus. Doge Dandolo stayed ashore near the beached and victorious galleys of Venice—for there could be no doubt that it was a Venetian triumph. The knights and Crusaders might have been responsible for breaking down the seaward gate and routing the Emperor's forces, but it was the Venetians who had got them there in the first place. It was the Venetian success against the two towers that had enabled the landing-parties to establish themselves on the beach, and it was Venetian ingenuity that had dreamed up the assault-ramps, without which the towers and walls would never have been taken.

The victors rested, but they most certainly expected that the day's triumph was no more than the end of the beginning. In view of the immensity of the city that lay sprawled in front of them (a city designed, it seemed, to be contested alley by alley, street by street and forum by forum), these veteran soldiers found it impossible to believe that Constantinople was already taken. In the morning they would wake to find that the unbelievable prize was theirs.

14

CONQUEST AND LOOT

THE God-guarded walls had failed them. The Sacred Ikon of Blachernae, containing the portrait of the Mother of God and a fragment of the Virgin's robe, the innumerable pieces of the Holy Cross, the head of John the Baptist, and the thousand and one relics of apostles, saints and martyrs had not been able to protect them. For the first time in 900 years the city of Constantine had been stormed and occupied by an enemy.

It was small wonder that the Byzantines, demoralised as they were already, had little or no spirit left. The common people who had briefly found a saviour in Murtzuphlus felt only that he had failed them, while the nobility who had conspired against him were eager to come to some advantageous arrangement with the conquerors. What difference could it make to them who ruled the city—so long as their own rights and privileges were observed? Perhaps, indeed, it would be better to have a man like Boniface as emperor, a man who could call upon Crusading swords to preserve the empire?

Ever since 1096 when Godfrey de Bouillon had led the First Crusade to Constantinople on its way through to Asia, the hardihood and vigour of the western Europeans had amazed and alarmed the Byzantines. They had attempted to channel the Crusaders for their own ends, and to use the tough soldiery of the West first to restore, and then to retain, their own dwindling eastern empire. Disappointed in this ambition, they had found themselves increasingly undermined by Venetian and Nòrman ambitions in Italy, Sicily and the Adriatic. Now they had suffered the final shame and indignity of being conquered by these Latins. But, some of them reasoned, if the Emperor himself should be a Latin, then the ancient Empire might itself be restored by western arms. Instead of wasting their energies in Outremer and Egypt, let these soldiers from Italy, Germany and France use them against the Turks in Asia Minor!

One thing was certain—Murtzuphlus could no longer count on any support from the common people and certainly not from the nobles. Early that evening, after his withdrawal to the Palace of Boucoleon, he was forced to the conclusion that his cause was hopeless. True, there was the Waring guard, always prepared to fight to the death, but they were no more than a comparative handful of men. The Byzantine troops themselves were demoralised, and subject to officers who felt no allegiance to Murtzuphlus. As the murderer of Alexius, the Crusaders' chosen emperor, he knew what his fate would be if he fell into their hands. There was nothing for him but to go while there was still a chance of escape. During that dark night, while the Golden Gate was open to permit a throng of people to fly from the city, Murtzuphlus left the palace. He joined the press of merchants and rich citizens who were driving out in heavily laden wagons from the doomed city. Murtzuphlus in his short reign had attempted the impossible: to put heart into an enfeebled people and to repair the ravages of nearly a century of decadent and cynical rulers. He had failed, but there was gallantry in his failure. He was, perhaps, the last Emperor of the ancient Byzantine Empire worthy to bear the name.

At this late hour Theodore Lascaris, the only other noble who had shown himself capable of nobility, made a last appeal to the people. It took him little time to realise the futility of his gesture. The city was already lost—not so much through the breach in its walls, as through the defeatist attitude of its citizens. Following the example of Murtzuphlus he, too, escaped from the city. But his choice of route was different. Instead of making his way south into Thrace, Theodore Lascaris took ship across the Bosphorus, and then made his way overland to Nicea. The most important Byzantine city in northern Asia Minor, Nicea on the lake of Ascania, was soon destined to become the seat of the Greek Byzantine Emperors.

"During that night," writes Villehardouin, "certain unknown individuals, afraid that the Greeks might attack them, set fire to the buildings between themselves and the enemy . . ." Thus began the third fire of Constantinople, the third holocaust for which the invaders were responsible. The works of art and of literature lost in these successive fires must in themselves be enough to brand the Fourth Crusade with infamy. Recalling sadly how much was destroyed even before the Crusaders had sacked and looted the city, Villehardouin remarked, "More houses were burnt in these fires than there are to be found in any of the three largest cities in France." Yet even after all this wanton destruction the city still dazzled the invaders with its size and splendour. Even after acres of it had been reduced to ashes, it was still grander and nobler than anything any of them had ever seen before.

"So the night passed and the next day came . . ." On Tuesday, April 13th, 1204, the combined forces of the Crusaders and the Venetians under Boniface, Marquis of Montferrat, and Enrico Dandolo, Doge of Venice, took possession of the greatest Christian city in the world. The Byzantine forces, under their supine leaders, formally laid down their arms. Even the Warings, totally confused as to whether there was still an emperor to whom they owed allegiance (or, if there was an emperor, who he was), at last submitted to the Latins.

The Marquis of Montferrat rode straight to the imperial palace of Boucoleon. This, as he knew, was the heart of Constantinople and the true seat of power. No one opposed him as he passed in triumph along the shore, followed by his armoured knights. In the palace they found the ladies of the court, among them the sister of the King of France, and the sister of the King of Hungary. So much gracious nobility could hardly fail to impress these simple barons. But what impressed them even more was, in Villehardouin's words, "the amount of treasure in that palace, so many precious things that one could not count them. Words fail me in any attempt to describe them!"

Meanwhile Henri of Flanders, brother of Baldwin, Count of Flanders, had received the formal surrender of the palace of

Blachernae. Words failed Villehardouin yet again when he tried to enumerate the treasures of the second imperial palace. But a simple Crusader's view of the aftermath of the surrender of the city was less enthusiastic. As Robert de Clari wrote: "Now all the rich and important men got together and decided between them to take for themselves the most important places in the city. They made their arrangements without letting the lesser folk know what they had in mind, let alone the poor foot soldiers in the army. It was from that moment on that they began to break faith with the rank and file and to forget their old companions. They set out to seize all the richest palaces— and so swiftly, that they had occupied them before the poorer knights or men-at-arms even realised what they were doing. But when the rest of the army finally saw what was afoot, they started to look after themselves and to lay their hands on whatsoever they could . . ." Thus began the sack of Constantinople and the spoliation of the richest city in Europe. It was the beginning of a shameful episode, a day that should be deep-edged in black in the church calendars of the western world. It was one of the greatest betrayals in history—a betrayal of their Crusading oaths, of the Christian faith and of the Byzantines who had laid down their arms and peacefully submitted their city.

Secure in the knowledge that the city was now in the hands of the invaders, the dispossessed Italian colonists who had been living in Galata ever since the second great fire, began to stream back across the water. Imbued with a hatred of the Byzantines who had driven them from their shops and houses, and confident that they had the protection of their fellow-countrymen and co-religionists, these Pisans and Genoese now took an ample revenge. As the monk Gunther tells us, they were the first to take arms against the Byzantines and they alone were responsible for killing nearly 2,000 Greeks. They had, as they felt, wrongs to be avenged against a city that had permitted Moslems to trade in rivalry with them, and many a grievance to be redressed against the trading community of Constantinople.

Despite de Clari's statement that the best of the houses and the loot was divided beforehand among the leaders of the expedition, the whole city lay defenceless before the army and they hastened to take advantage of it. In Villehardouin's words, "The army spread through the city and began to loot it: and they took more than anyone can calculate. They seized gold and silver, precious stones and tableware of precious metals, silks and satins, coats of fur—squirrel, ermine and miniver—and indeed all the riches of the earth. I, Geoffrey de Villehardouin, stake my word that never had any army gained so much plunder in the whole history of the world . . ."

While a procession of Orthodox priests made their formal acknowledgement to the conquerors, the citizens knelt in the streets as the mounted Crusaders spurred by. Placing one forefinger over another in the sign of the Cross, these eastern Christians attempted to remind the westerners that they were members of the same faith. There were still many—particularly among the rich and powerful—who believed that the advent of Boniface of Montferrat could only be the salvation of their city and themselves. These men who had all along opposed Murtzuphlus (and among them one must count the historian Nicetas) had never before seen the Berserker fury of a western European army when it was unleashed upon a city that had been taken by siege. They were still innocent enough to believe that all that was happening was, as it were, a change of ruler. They had seen emperors come and go, and they were under the illusion that they were about to receive a Latin emperor—and no more. This ingenuous belief was to be shattered within a few dreadful hours.

Describing the entry of the Persians into Europe many centuries before, A. R. Burn writes: "Greed is not usually an important ingredient in a conqueror's character. The famous conqueror inevitably possesses or controls, before he is in mid-career, the means to luxury beyond the most gargantuan powers of consumption. Moreover, the great man of action, even 'the great bad man', is often personally austere. But avarice may be a very important motive in the 'average, sensual' poor men, who jump on the band-wagon and form a conqueror's armies; which is why the thesis of the importance of economic, material motives is not controverted by insistence on the idealism or personal austerity of the leader . . ."*

There was no great conqueror involved in the siege and capture of Constantinople. The opportunist Doge of Venice, Enrico Dandolo, had indeed master-minded the conflicting ambitions of a number of men to serve his own interests—and those of his state. But there was no real controlling influence or authority over the invaders as a whole. The Venetians were still under the penalty of excommunication by Pope Innocent, and most of the Crusaders had long ago dispensed with their Crusading oaths. Once released upon the city, the army became no more than a rabble inflamed by lust and greed.

When the Russians had attacked the city in the ninth century the Patriarch Photius had seen this threat to Constantinople as a divine visitation for the wrongdoings of its inhabitants: "We enjoyed ourselves and grieved others. We were glorified and dishonoured others. We grew strong and throve, while waxing insolent and foolish . . . For these reasons there is a sound of war and destruction in the land." But the Russians had been driven back in defeat. It was only now, three centuries later, that the prophecies were fulfilled—not least those ominous words to be found in the Book of Revelation:

"And the merchants of the earth shall weep and mourn over her; for no man buyeth their merchandise any more: the merchandise of gold, and silver, and precious stones, and of pearls, and fine linen, and purple, and silk, and scarlet, and all thyine wood, and all manner vessels of ivory, and all manner vessels of most precious wood, and of brass, and iron, and marble, and cinnamon, and odours, and ointments, and frankincense, and wine, and oil, and fine flour, and wheat, and beasts, and sheep, and horses, and chariots, and slaves, and souls of men. And the fruits that thy soul lusted after are departed from thee, and all things which were dainty and goodly are departed from thee, and thou shalt find them no more at all. The merchants of these things, which were made rich by her, shall stand afar off for the fear of her torment, weeping and wailing, and saying, Alas, alas, that great city, that was clothed in fine linen, and purple, and scarlet, and decked with gold, and precious stones, and pearls! For in one hour so great riches is come to nought. And every shipmaster, and all the company in ships, and sailors, and as many as trade by sea, stood afar off, and cried when they saw the smoke of her burning, saying, What city is like unto this great city!"

Seventeen times in the past nine centuries the city had come under the attack of its enemies and seventeen times it had survived, lifting the proud line of its unconquered walls above the smoke of battle, the thunder of siege-engines and the snorting fury of Greek fire. Now it had fallen ignominiously, captured by a comparatively minor assault that had left untouched the splendour of the Theodosian walls to the west and the great sea-ramparts scowling above the Marmora.

"But now that the city was ours our men took up their quarters where they pleased for there were innumerable fine houses in the city. All of us gave thanks to God for the victory and rejoiced, for even those of us who had been poor now lived in wealth and comfort..." Thus Villehardouin, but the 'wealth and comfort' were not arrived at without brutality and terror. The uncontestably true story of the sack of Constantinople is given by Nicetas and Gunther, and it is amply confirmed by the famous letter which Innocent III later wrote denouncing the conquest and sack of the city.

Nicetas, who had perhaps looked for a solution to his country's difficulties from the Crusaders, and who certainly had no love either for Murtzuphlus or the previous two emperors, said of the Crusaders' crimes that "They had taken up the Cross and had sworn on it and on the Holy Gospels that they would pass over the lands of the Christians without shedding blood and without turning to the right hand or the left. They had told us that they had taken up arms against the Saracens only and that they would steep them in their blood alone. They had promised to keep themselves chaste while they bore the Cross as befitted soldiers of Christ. But instead of defending His tomb, they had outraged the faithful who are members of Him. They used Christians worse than the Arabs use Latins, for at least the Arabs respected women."

Even in a century when men have grown numbed by atrocities, the story of the sack of Constantinople must cause a sigh of despair at the stupidity and inhumanity of man. "They respected nothing," cries Nicetas, "neither the churches, nor the sacred images of Christ and his Saints! They acted like enemies of the Cross! They committed atrocities upon men, respectable women, virgins, and young girls!"

Monasteries and convents were sacked and looted, nuns raped, and even the sacred precincts of Santa Sophia, noblest cathedral in Christendom, were invaded by hordes of drunken rapacious soldiery. They rode their horses into the great sanctuary of the Divine Wisdom and tore the very vestments from the priests at the altar. Not content with profaning that shrine, the majesty of whose surroundings and awe-inspiring mosaics of Christ Pantocrator and his Virgin Mother should have stilled their hearts, they broke up the altars for the sake of their marbles and gold and silver. The wealth of sacred vessels which had been accumulating in the cathedral throughout nine centuries was seized upon by soldiers ignorant of everything save that they might be melted down and converted into coin. Frames and settings were ripped from priceless ikons so that the gold in them might be melted down and the gemstones sold. The art of the enameller which had been brought to its greatest peak of perfection by Byzantine craftsmen meant nothing to ignorant soldiers. Enamelled vessels, reliquaries, book covers, chalices and patens were eagerly seized upon for the weight of precious metal they contained.

Only the Venetians amid the wild sack of the city seemed to have retained some sense of values. They hunted in organised bands through the churches and private houses for objects that might be used to grace their own city of the canals. Nearly all the thirty-two chalices now in the Treasury of St. Mark's were taken from Constantinople. The magnificent cloisonné enamelled reliquary containing a relic of the True Cross—one of the principal prides of St. Mark's—is yet another piece of loot from the sack.

Not content with ransacking and desecrating Santa Sophia, the Crusaders showed their contempt for eastern Christendom by enthroning a common whore in the Patriarchal chair. "Then, to show her contempt, she danced and sang lewd songs, dishonouring the name of God . . ."

Not for nearly six centuries, not indeed until 1793, when the French mob sacked their own churches, would Europe witness anything comparable to the desecration of Santa Sophia and the other churches of Constantinople: "Most of these persons were still drunk with the brandy they had swallowed out of chalices; eating mackerel on patenas! Mounted on asses, which were housed with priest's cloaks, they reined them with priests' stoles; they held clutched with the same hand communion-cup and sacred wafer. They stopped at the doors of Dramshops; held out ciboriums: and the landlord, stoop in hand, had to fill them thrice. Next came mules high-laden with crosses, chandeliers, censers, holy-water vessels, hyssops: recalling to mind the Priests of Cybele, whose panniers, filled with the instruments of their worship, served at once as storehouse, sacristy and temple. In such equipage did these profiteers advance . . . in an immense train, ranged in two rows; all masked like mummers in fantastic sacerdotal vestments; bearing on hand-barrows their heaped plunder, ciboriums, suns, candelabras, plates of gold and silver."*

Never in history had there been anything to equal the loot that now fell into the hands of these soldiers of the Fourth Crusade. Robert de Clari's description of the palaces and the chapels and houses of the city reads like a gasp of wonder: "In the palace of Boucoleon which the Marquis of Montferrat occupied, there were five hundred rooms, the one leading into the other, and all of them decorated with gold mosaic work. There were at least thirty chapels in the palace, some large and some small. Most outstanding of all was the Holy Chapel where even the door hinges and nails and things that are normally made of iron were all of silver. Not a column in it but was of jasper or porphyry or of precious stone! The chapel's pavement was of white marble so polished and shining that one might have taken it for crystal. I cannot begin to tell you how beautiful and grand this whole building was! We found many rich relics here, among them two pieces of the True Cross, as thick as a man's leg and about three feet long. Then there was the iron head of the lance which pierced Our Lord's side, and the nails which were struck through His hands and feet, a phial containing some of His blood, and the tunic that He wore . . ."

All of these relics and hundreds more like them were soon to be dispersed throughout Europe, so that there was hardly a church or chapel of any importance in France or Italy which was not soon to be endowed with some miraculous and wonder-working object, bone or vestment. It was the Age of Faith (which later centuries might equate with the Age of Super-stition), but, nevertheless, to these medieval Christians the tangible evidences of the saints and martyrs, and of the Holy Family itself, were the buttresses of that Faith. Constantinople, had become through the ages an immense repository of such relics, collected from all the Near East. The flow of them to the capital had steadily increased as the Moslems had invaded areas that were formerly Christian. The first thing that occurred to priests fleeing from towns and cities about to fall into Moslem hands was to save the evidences of their faith. From the fall of Alexandria to the Arabs in the seventh century, throughout the gradual loss of eastern Christendom, the stream of relics into Constantinople had increased to a flood—especially since the eleventh century as the Turks occupied Asia Minor and as so many old centres of Christian worship fell into their hands.

Although three-eighths of the relics in the city were officially allotted to the clergy, it was not only the Catholic priests who scavenged through the churches, monasteries and convents. The knights, men-at-arms and common soldiers were equally superstitious, and undoubtedly many of them felt that only by obtaining possession of some holy relic might their crime of having attacked the city be assuaged. The man who could return to his home town or parish with the shin-bone of a martyr, or some really important relic like the head of a saint, was certain of being freed from the terrors of excommunication and of being welcomed back in honour to his church. Such a one was Dalmatius de Sergy, who managed to steal the head of

St. Clement from the church of St. Theodosia, and later presented it to the monks of Cluny. The Bishop of Soissons, for his part, managed to take back dozens of relics to his own See—among them the arm of John the Baptist, the head of St. Stephen, and the finger which doubting Thomas thrust into the side of Our Lord. Like works of art by famous old masters, relics proliferated suspiciously. There was to be argument for centuries to come about the authenticity of certain relics from the sack of Constantinople—particularly when it was discovered, for instance, that there was more than one head of John the Baptist in existence.

While France, Germany and Italy contrived to secure more relics than any other countries, loot from Constantinople even found its way to churches in remote England. Such sacred objects gave their possessors a unique position in those days when pilgrimages to shrines played an important part in religious life. In this way, Bromholm in Norfolk was to become prosperous from pilgrimages made to the 'Sacred Rood of Bromholm'—a fragment of the True Cross carved into the shape of a cross, and stolen by an unknown soldier (presumably English) from Count Baldwin of Flanders in 1204.

It was Venice, above all, which benefited from the relics seized during the sack of the city. While it was the sacred relic inside its case or covering which gave the object its value in medieval Christian eyes, the reliquary containing the object was more often than not a marvellous work of art. The dispersion of so many almost miraculous objects of jewellery and enamel to Venice served to promote these crafts in the city, as her native craftsmen strove to emulate the Byzantines. In this way, throughout hundreds of cities in Europe, local artisans were prompted to try and rival the master-craftsmen and artists of Constantinople.

Although historians in the nineteenth century—and even subsequently—have claimed that the sack of Constantinople by the Turks in the fifteenth century unleashed a flood of works of art and of artists upon Europe—thus promoting the Renaissance—this simple assumption must be dismissed. It was the Latin conquest of the city in 1204 which first began the great dispersal not only of works of art but also of Byzantine artists and craftsmen throughout western Europe. It was from them that so many European jewellers, enamellers, gemsetters and modellers first learned what could be achieved with precious metals, ivories, gemstones and enamels.

Outstanding works of art like the cover of a reliquary for the preservation of a fragment of the True Cross (now to be seen at Limburg an der Lahn, Germany) reached a nunnery at Stuben shortly after the sack of the city. Set with half-pearls and with cabochon-cut gemstones, this masterpiece of gold and enamel was, like many others, to influence future generations of metal-workers and to give them an ideal towards which to aspire. As Professor Talbot Rice has remarked: "It was really as a result of the immense influx of Byzantine works of art brought after 1204 as loot accumulated by the Fourth Crusade that the imitation of Byzantine objects began on a really wide scale, and it was then that Venice became really active as a centre for the production of works in metal and enamel, and even stone, in a basically Byzantine style, so that it is sometimes hard to tell the Venetian copies from the Byzantine originals ..."*

A curious fact which emerges from the looting of thousands of relics from Constantinople is that the Crusaders venerated them far more than did the Orthodox Greek Christians. A sceptical spirit has always been part of Greek nature, and although many of the faithful regarded these objects with awe and devotion, most Byzantines did not suffer from the same credulity as did the western Europeans of this date. With the instinctive Greek reverence for visual beauty they regarded the ikons and their bejewelled frames, the church furniture, the enamelled bindings of sacred books and the reliquaries them-selves, with as much reverence as the objects they were said to contain.

But if a superstitious regard for relics blinded the Crusaders to the aesthetic value of their containers, the splendour of the ornaments and objects of everyday life in Constantinople excited their greed. Robert de Clari can find only one adjective to describe the treasure of Boucoleon Palace: "One found there a vast wealth of richness, for there were the rich crowns which had belonged to previous emperors, and rich jewels of gold, and rich garments of silk embroidered with gold, and rich imperial robes, and rich precious stones. Indeed there were so many rich things that one could hardly count the huge treasure of gold and silver to be found in the palace as well as in many other places in the city."

15

DEATH OF A CITY

"Now among all the marvels of the city the most astounding
were two columns. Each was at least the span of a man's
outstretched arms in width, and about three hundred feet high.
On top of these were small dwellings where hermits used to live,
and there were staircases inside the columns so that one could
climb up to them. On the outside of the columns there were
prophetic pictures and writings, showing all the events and all
the conquests which have ever happened at Constantinople, or
which are ever going to happen. Now no one could understand
an event until it had happened, but afterwards people would go
and look at the prophetic writings and pictures and then they
would suddenly see and understand it. Even this present French
conquest of the city was depicted and described on the columns
—right down to the very ships in which they had made their
attack on the city. The Greeks, however, had not been able to
understand it beforehand. But now that they went and looked
at the columns, they found letters inscribed on these ships,
which said that a race would come out of the West, who would
wear their hair long and carry iron swords, and that they would
capture Constantinople!"

Robert de Clari's account of the city in those last days has all
the simple wonder of the eternal tourist. Villehardouin, on the
other hand, while marvelling at 'the sights' was more pre-
occupied with policy. It is clear that in his old age he regretted
the way in which the leaders of the army had lost their control
over the troops. It is he who tells us that, for three whole days,
Constantinople was given over to sack and massacre. It was
not until the third day that even the Catholic bishops who had

travelled with the Crusaders ventured to pronounce sentence of excommunication upon those who should plunder church, convent or monastery, or lay hands upon any of the priests, monks and nuns of the Orthodox Faith.

Although the loss to the world of so much unique Christian art—melted down, torn to pieces for its gems or burnt in the wanton firing of the city—is incalculable, it is the loss of the great works of art surviving from the pagan world that must appal the modern historian and art-lover. It was true that Constantinople was the city where the glorious monotheistic Nicene creed had been accepted since A.D. 326: "We believe in one God, the Father Almighty, Maker of heaven and earth, and of all things visible and invisible: and in One Lord Jesus Christ, the only-begotten Son of God, begotten of His Father before all worlds, Light of Light, Very God of Very God, begotten not made, being of one substance with the Father . . ." But the same people who embraced the Nicene creed were happy to tolerate, and indeed to love, the many evidences within their walls of the ancient world that had existed before ever the Crucified Saviour had died in an eastern province of the Roman Empire. Just as it abounded in Christian relics and reliquaries, the city was also the last treasure-trove of classical art in the world. Here the marbles and bronzes of great Greek and Roman sculptures formed a part of everyday life—an accepted background to the city.

One of these master-works was an immense bronze statue of Hercules, by the famous Greek sculptor Lysippus. Lysippus had been head of the school of Argos and Sicyon in the time of Alexander the Great. He worked only in bronze, became court sculptor to Alexander, and made many portrait statues of him. The Hercules, which had been brought to Constantinople from Tarentum in Italy, was accounted one of the finest bronzes surviving from the wreck of the ancient world. It was Lysippus who had modified the old conception of Hercules as no more than an arrogant 'strong man', and who had first depicted him as weary of the immense tasks he had undertaken, and scornful of their unworthy nature. His colossal bronze in Constantinople showed the hero seated, his lion-skin draped over his shoulders.

His left knee was bent and his head rested upon his left hand, the elbow on the knee, while his right leg and arm were stretched out to their full extent. The figure was august yet full of lassitude—it might have been taken as symbolic of the city itself, of its eternal struggle to clear up the Augean stables of the world. But the ignorant roaring mob who were now let loose upon the city had no interest in works of art—what concerned them was the bronze itself, so useful for turning into coin. The Hercules of Lysippus was dragged away, broken up and thrown into the melting-pots.

Another mammoth bronze to suffer a similar fate depicted Bellerophon mounted on Pegasus, one hand flung wide to the sky as if to command the sun to stand still. "It was so large," de Clari tells us, "that between the crupper and the horse's head there were ten herons' nests, and the birds came back there every year to nest and lay their eggs..." Neither its beauty nor its size saved it from destruction. The colossal figure of the Hera of Samos, which had long dominated the forum of Constantine, suffered a similar fate. It was in the island of Samos that the two sculptors Rhoecus and Theodorus were said to have invented the art of bronze casting, and this statue was the masterpiece which had graced the great temple of Hera, founded by the tyrant Polycrates in the sixth century B.C. The "ox-eyed, flower-bearing" Queen of the classical Heaven was soon no more than molten bronze to be recast as ingots and coins.

One of the marvels of Constantinople which had fascinated generations of travellers and visitors to the city was the Anemodoulion, the Servant of the Winds. This was the bronze figure of a woman set upon a tall obelisk. The statue was so perfectly balanced upon a revolving sphere that it swung and pointed in the direction of the wind. The sides of the obelisk were carved with bronze bas-reliefs depicting country scenes, rural festivities and the procession of the seasons of the year. Like ants picking clean a corpse, the troops swarmed all over the obelisk with ropes and tackles, pickaxes and crowbars. Soon nothing was left but a stone column pointing like a finger to the sky. The wind blew free over the bare top of the obelisk, where for so many centuries its Servant had twisted and turned, marking the onset of winter northerlies or the Sirocco blowing up in autumn from the Sea of Marmora.

Relics of ancient Rome, which subsequent generations would have given incalculable sums to be able to see and admire, were torn down and dragged off in handcarts to the greedy furnaces. The bronze statue of the she-wolf suckling Romulus and Remus, which had been one of the sacred monuments of ancient Rome, was borne away. Paris presenting the apple to Venus, and a famous bronze group which the Emperor Augustus had had cast to commemorate his victory over Antony and Cleopatra at the battle of Actium—these, too, were dragged off to the furnaces.

Nothing deterred the vandals. They did not destroy the idols and images of the ancient world out of any religious fanaticism. Their own Faith was equally desecrated, and a bronze statue of the Mother of God, long the focal point in the Forum of the Ox, was broken up and melted down. They had as little regard for it as for the great bronze charioteers—monuments to famous victors in the races—which they hauled away from the eastern end of the Hippodrome.

Meanwhile the fire continued to sweep through the rich quarter of the city between the Golden Horn and Mesé Street. It will never be known what treasures were lost in this and the previous two fires—what manuscripts from the classical world, what monuments of Byzantine art, painted ikons, illuminated manuscripts, and copies of the gospels and other religious works. In the roaring heat of the wood-fired blaze, marbles cracked and disintegrated and painted walls went up in smoke. Mosaic ceilings fell in as the inlaid pieces of marble, enamel and glass fell away from the liquefying bitumen that had held them in place. Walls and ceilings made of gold tesserae shrilled to the ground, as the twin layers of glass that held the gold-leaf intact cracked in the intense heat. Enamels ran like tears from images of the Virgin and of the Saints.

Through the crumbling ruins of the city scurried the greed-obsessed, lust-filled figures of the Crusaders. Here a group of men carried off one of the most curious bronzes of history—

curious, for it was the work of a philosopher, the Saintly Apollonius of Tyana. He had depicted the force of good triumphing over evil in the shape of an eagle destroying a snake. It had reached Constantinople from Ephesus, where Apollonius (a mystic who had reconciled the spiritual beliefs of the Orient with the doctrines of Pythagoras) had died in his hundredth year. Born before Christ, Apollonius had outlived the Messiah by nearly half a century, had been acclaimed with divine honours, and had been hailed by many pagans as greater than his Hebrew predecessor.

In another part of the city a statue of Helen of Troy, dating from the finest period of Greek art, was dragged away to be broken up. "Fairer than the evening air, clad in the beauty of a thousand stars", this statue caused Nicetas to lament: "Why could not Helen with her white arms and lovely form soften the hearts of the barbarians? Formerly she had made captive everyone who looked at her. She was clothed in a robe that hardly concealed her body but enhanced its beauty. Her forehead was high, and her hair seemed to move in an invisible wind. Her eyebrows were arched, and her lips looked as if she was just on the point of speaking. I do not possess the art to describe her adequately to those who now will never see her. She was all harmony, grace and elegance, and had been a delight to the eye of all who had ever beheld her."

If the sublimity of great works of art could not move the heart of the conquerors, it was unlikely that the living bodies of the despised Byzantines would be treated with any kindness or charity. Slaughter and rapine was the order of the day. "On all sides there was nothing to be heard but cries, groans, laments and screams. Here there were fights and quarrels over loot, there prisoners were being led away, and everywhere among the raped and the wounded lay the dead . . ."

The story of how Nicetas himself escaped from the city must be typical of what happened to many others. His own large house had been burned to the ground in the second great fire. Now Nicetas was not only a Byzantine nobleman but had held the office of Great Logothete, so one may well believe him when he sighs over the loss of innumerable works of art and other treasures from his personal collection. After this disaster he and his family had been hidden by a Venetian merchant and his family in a small house near Santa Sophia. The reason for this act of kindness was that Nicetas himself had helped and hidden the Venetian in exactly the same way at the time when the Latins were being expelled from the city. A group of Nicetas's friends also took refuge with him, but finally their protector was no longer able to conceal his distinguished guests and there was nothing for it but for all of them to try and make their escape. Nicetas describes how his own daughters and several other young women in the group were dressed in rags, with their faces disfigured by dirt, so as to try and save them from the lust of the soldiers. Even so, as the small party was making its way out of the city, one of the young women (the daughter of a magistrate) was seized by a passing soldier. Her father, who was old and feeble, could do nothing to help and it was only the efforts of the historian himself that saved her. Nicetas pleaded with a group of passing soldiers and reminded them of their oath to respect the women of the city. His eloquence led them to restore the magistrate's daughter, and to threaten to hang the Crusader who had tried to violate her.

As Nicetas and his friends left Constantinople they saw on all sides of them scenes of unbridled lust and cruelty, while the sight of the burning city filled their hearts with unspeakable anguish. Making their way south towards Selymbria in northern Thrace they saw among the stream of refugees in front of them the Patriarch of Constantinople himself. "Like a true follower of Jesus Christ he had neither money nor shoes, but rode out wearing but a single coat, and mounted on an ass. What so sadly distinguished him from the apostles of old was that, far from entering the New Jerusalem in triumph, he was leaving it behind him."

They turned and took one last look at the great landward walls and the Golden Gate. Behind the defences, the roofs of palaces and houses and churches lifted above a haze of smoke. Were there any, among these nobles and church dignitaries who were now fleeing the city, who remembered the words of the Empress Theodora to Justinian when he was contemplating flight after the famous Nika Rebellion seven centuries before? "I hold," she had said, "that now, if ever, flight is inexpedient even if it brings safety. When a man has once been born into the light it is inevitable that he should also meet death. But for an Emperor to become a fugitive is not a thing to be endured ... Royalty makes a fine winding-sheet."

For most of these fugitives this was the last sight that they would ever have of "Byzantium radiant in a blaze of gold". For the rest of their lives they would remember with tears the Incomparable City. But the Constantinople for which they would mourn was already dead. Together with the Byzantine Empire it had ceased to exist on that fateful morning of Monday April 12th, 1204, when the Venetians and the Crusaders had breached the sea-walls on the Golden Horn. For two and a half centuries more it would lie, framed by its blue waters, a ravished and plundered husk awaiting extinction.

16

THE TRIUMPH OF VENICE

AFTER three days the leaders of the army seem suddenly to have realised that they were destroying their inheritance. Order must be restored so that the formal collection and distribution of the plunder could take place. The Venetians must be paid, and that fatal debt which had been overhanging the Crusaders for the past three years must be discharged. From now on discipline was the order of the day and, as Villehardouin tells us, "The Count of Saint-Paul had one of his own knights hanged, with his shield suspended from his neck, for concealing treasure that should have gone into the common fund..."

Three churches had been set aside as collecting points for the loot. The conquerors appear to have felt no shame in thus converting churches into depositories for plunder (much of it taken from other churches). It did not occur to them that they were offending their God even more than the money-changers whom Jesus had driven out of the temple in Jerusalem. Indeed, the words of Jesus as reported by St. Matthew were singularly applicable to the Crusaders: "And he said unto them, It is written, My house shall be called the house of prayer; but ye have made it a den of thieves."

The plunder that had been brought into the churches was now divided equally between the Crusaders and the Venetians, as had been agreed before the assault on the city. Out of the Crusaders' share, 50,000 silver marks was immediately handed over to the Venetians to discharge their debt to them, and a further 100,000 marks was then divided among the troops. "A mounted sergeant," Villehardouin tells us, "received twice as much as a foot sergeant, while a knight received twice as much as two mounted sergeants. No one, whoever we might be, received any more unless there was some special arrangement—or unless he happened to steal it."

Of course the term 'special arrangement' may well have covered a multitude of sins while, as we know, an incredible amount of treasure had already been stolen by private individuals. But even allowing for all this, the total value of the plunder was in the region of 400,000 silver marks as well as some 10,000 horses. An early nineteenth-century calculation of the wealth in Constantinople in coin and property before the conquest gives a figure of £24,000,000.* Sir Edwin Pears writing in the late nineteenth century commented that "the total amount distributed among the Crusaders and Venetians shows that the wealth of Constantinople had not been exaggerated. £80,000 was given to the Crusaders, a like sum to the Venetians, together with the £100,000 due to them. These sums had been collected in hard cash from a city where the inhabitants were hostile, and where they had in their wells and cisterns an easy means of hiding their treasures of gold, silver and precious stones—a means traditionally well known in the East—and in a city *half of which had been recently burned in three great fires.*"* In terms of modern currency it would seem that not less than £6,000,000 was officially divided in coin between the Crusaders and Venetians. This does not take into account the enormous, but unknown, quantity of money and valuables which were stolen.

The systematic looting of Constantinople for relics went on for years after the conquest, so that before very long there was hardly a cathedral, monastery or church of any importance in western Europe, which did not contain some enamelled and bejewelled reliquary dating from the sack of the city. Venice itself is a monument to the Fourth Crusade. It was the Venetian acquisition of, in Dandolo's own phrase, "a half and a quarter of the Roman Empire" that truly established the city's fortunes. The Treasury of St. Mark's contains the finest collection of Byzantine craftsmanship in the world, nearly all of it stemming from loot brought back after April 1204. The famous Pala d'Oro, the retable of the high altar within which rests the body of St. Mark—one of the greatest examples of the goldsmiths' and jewellers' craft in existence—was largely a Byzantine work of the early twelfth century. It contains, however, numerous pieces of Byzantine enamel work taken from Constantinople in 1204. These were set into the retable when it was enlarged and modified in 1209. The finest Byzantine ivory casket in the world, the Veroli casket, so-called from its having belonged to the Cathedral Treasury of Veroli near Rome, may also have reached Italy after the sack of Constantinople.*

The dissemination of Byzantine works of art throughout Europe provided the springboard which later helped to launch the Renaissance. Although metal-workers, artists, mosaic-workers, textile-designers and other craftsmen from Constantinople had long been active in the Italian world, their home and the home of their guilds had always—until the Latin conquest—been the Greek city on the Bosphorus. After the sack many of them left, never to return. The gradual diffusion of Byzantine learning and artistry continued throughout the next two and a half centuries, until the Turkish conquest of the city wrote an end to a unique Christian civilisation.

Now that the plunder was divided, and all parties were satisfied financially, there remained the pressing and important problem of electing a new emperor and of dividing those more permanent spoils—the actual land heritage of Byzantium. There were three obvious candidates for emperor, Boniface Marquis of Montferrat, Baldwin Earl of Flanders and, inevitably, Enrico Dandolo. The latter had no wish to take on the responsibilities of emperor. He was Doge of Venice already, and he saw quite clearly what kind of cat's cradle of politics and policy would be handed over to the first non-Greek, non-Orthodox emperor of the city. In any case, Dandolo was over eighty years old. If he had distinguished himself by controlling the puppets of the Fourth Crusade, he had no intention of ending his life as the puppet of others. Quite apart from his age, he may well have doubted whether he would receive much support. The Crusaders—now that the city was theirs—could allow their natural resentment against the Venetians to come to the surface. The Venetians, on the other hand, would hardly welcome one of their own citizens as the ruler of Constantinople, with the possibility that he might found a dynasty in the East. Venice was a republic, the Venetians had curbed the power of the Doges in the early eleventh century and they had an inborn distaste for the trappings of monarchy.

Dandolo was wise and did not put himself forward as a candidate. He knew that he could wield far more power behind the scenes, and his own interests coincided with those of his city. It was the trade of Constantinople which interested Venice, and—to secure that trade—certain islands and ports in the Ionian, the Aegean and the Levant. It was, above all, the islands of the Aegean which had once proved the stepping-stones between Europe and Asia for Athens—and subsequently for the Byzantine Empire—that were of interest to Venice. Here lay the harbours and the seamen who could further Venetian trade. It was of little consequence who (technically) owned large areas of impoverished Greece and Turk-threatened Asia.

There were two main candidates, then, for the most ancient throne in Europe—Boniface, Marquis of Montferrat, and Baldwin, Earl of Flanders. No one else among the assembled Crusaders approached them either in rank, or in general distinction. The whole army was summoned to a conference and at this first meeting, "the main source of disagreement was whether Count Baldwin or the Marquis should be chosen . . .".

Aware that the choice of one as emperor might well cause the other to withdraw all his men from the army, and possibly even lead to a civil war, the council of the barons together with the Doge and the leading Venetians came to the conclusion that some worthwhile 'consolation prize' must be given to the loser.

"Whichever of them is elected," they said, "let him do everything he can to keep the other satisfied. A good way, for instance, for the new Emperor to gain the other's allegiance would be to grant him all the land that lies over the strait in Asia Minor, as well as the island of Greece [Crete]." Both contestants for the title agreed to this division of the Empire, and it was arranged that the Latins and Venetians should each choose six electors. These would meet in due course in May and would then decide who was to be the Emperor of Constantinople.

During the weeks that followed, the lobbying for candidates reached a fever-pitch of intrigue and counter-intrigue. There were still some who wished to see the Doge made emperor, but he had made his own views clear on this subject. There can be little doubt, though, that he was the presiding spirit in directing the course of the forthcoming election. At first glance it might have seemed that the weight of the Doge's authority would be cast in favour of Boniface. The latter was an Italian, he had been appointed the official leader of the Fourth Crusade, and he had systematically intrigued with Dandolo to divert the expedition to Constantinople. Their mutual aims had now been achieved, and together they had reached a triumphant conclusion—the sack of the richest city in Europe and the dismemberment of the Byzantine Empire.

Boniface had other assets to recommend him: he was recognised as a valiant and able soldier; he had the appearance and authority suitable for his position (his nickname was 'The Giant'); and the citizens of Constantinople were prepared to acclaim him as their new ruler. Furthermore, as if to ensure his claim to the throne, he had paid his court to Margaret, the widow of the Emperor Isaac and the sister of the King of Hungary. Their marriage was arranged to take place in the first week of May, just prior to the election.

Baldwin of Flanders, on the other hand, seemed to have much less to recommend him. True, he was the cousin of the King of France and descended from the great Charlemagne— a fact which appealed to the Latin Crusaders—but he did not have the energy and fire which distinguished Boniface. He was a genial man, however, and popular with the troops. Once the diversion of the Crusade had been accomplished, he had sided wholeheartedly with Dandolo and Boniface. But the fact remained that he had not been privy to the original plot, and this might well make him more acceptable in the Pope's eyes as the first new Latin emperor.

If the Doge now threw the weight of his authority behind Baldwin rather than Boniface, it can only have been that he envisaged Boniface as likely to be too powerful and too ambitious an emperor. Having destroyed any Byzantine threat to his own Republic, the Doge could have had no wish to see the ancient Empire reconstituted in a far more efficient form than before. Besides, it would not suit Venice to have a strong alliance between an Italian power and Constantinople—to have, in fact, an emperor in Constantinople whose sway extended as far as the Marquisate of Montferrat to the north of Venice. Count Baldwin, on the other hand, was quite a different proposition. His lands were far away in Flanders, and the fact that the territories which bore allegiance to him would be so widely separated would ensure that no power-combine could be erected that would in any way conflict with Venetian interests. Furthermore, the fact that Baldwin tended to be easy-going and tolerant meant that his ambitions would probably be assuaged, while Boniface, on the other hand, might not be so easily satisfied.

"Finally the day of the last conference arrived and everyone assembled. The twelve electors were chosen, six Latins and six Venetians, and all of them swore on the Holy Gospels to be conscientious and true in their work, and to elect the man who would best fulfil his duties to the state and the Empire..." It was arranged that the election itself should take place on May 9th in the Church of Our Lady inside Boucoleon Palace.

The day came, the electors met, and almost at once dissension broke out. Far from there being a simple argument between the merits or demerits of Boniface and Baldwin, the names of other alternative emperors were put up for consideration. Two of the Latin electors, the Bishops of Soissons and of Troyes, voted for Dandolo, although there is no indication that his name had ever been submitted. The bishops felt no doubt that, as he had proved himself the undisputed leader and organiser of the expedition, so it was only fitting that he should take charge of the conquered city and its territories. Others proposed that Philip of Swabia, whose name had never previously been mentioned in this connection, should be made emperor. They pointed out that, since he was likely to become Emperor of the West, it was only right that the two political divisions of

Christendom should now be united under one head—just as in
the spiritual sphere the Pope had now become sole ruler of the
Christian Church. The remainder of the electors seem to have
remained equally divided between Boniface and Baldwin.

The deliberations reached such an impasse that there seemed
only one recourse: to summon an outside authority to help the
electors make up their minds. Since Boniface and Baldwin were
committed parties, it was inevitable that they should turn to the
Doge. Disclaiming at once any desire to have the honour for
himself—thus silencing the two Bishops who had proposed him
—the Doge ignored also the supporters of Philip of Swabia.
The very idea of Philip becoming emperor of both East and
West must have appalled Dandolo. Nothing could have been
further from the designs of Venice than that a German Emperor
should possibly consolidate a vast empire stretching from the
Rhine to the Bosphorus. There were only two possible candidates, the Doge pointed out, and he proceeded to throw his
influence solidly in favour of Baldwin.*

"Meanwhile the barons and the knights waited in the great
palace outside the church..." That the election was not
rigged, but genuinely debated, must be judged from the fact
that the twelve electors were inside the church for many hours,
and it was not until close on midnight that they all emerged.
The Bishop of Soissons, who had been chosen as their spokesman, led the electors in front of the Doge and the other barons,
who were seated in one of the great reception rooms of
Boucoleon.

"My Lords," said the bishop, "we have by God's Grace
agreed on the choice of an Emperor. All of you have likewise
agreed to abide by our decision and, if anyone should dare
challenge it, to rally to the support of the man whom we have
elected. We name him now at midnight, at that very hour when
Our Lord was born, and we proclaim as Emperor of Constantinople, Count Baldwin of Flanders and Hainault."

It was the hour of triumph for Dandolo and for Venice.
Constantinople, her greatest rival, had been sacked—and many
of the city's finest treasures would go to glorify the Republic.
An emperor had been elected who was unlikely to prove any

threat to Venetian aspirations in the Aegean and the Levant. The Crusaders had been successfully and for ever diverted from any enterprise against Egypt—with the result that the Venetians had fulfilled any obligations to Egypt's Sultan, and might now expect to benefit by the trading concessions he had promised them in Alexandria.

All that now remained was to divide and dismember the eastern empire, taking for Venice whatever islands and ports might ensure her lifeline to Asia and the Orient. As for these Crusaders, it was more than likely that whatever territories they seized they would be unable to rule them efficiently, let alone in unison with one another. "Divide and rule," the traditional policy of ancient Rome, was now to be applied by Venice to Rome's successor, the city of Constantine.

17

DISMEMBERMENT OF AN EMPIRE

On May 16th, 1204, seven days after the electors had given their decision, Count Baldwin was crowned Emperor in Santa Sophia. He had been borne aloft on a shield in the ancient manner, then conducted in a formal procession to the Cathedral, and was now to be crowned in a confused mixture of the rites of the Orthodox and Latin churches. Since the Greek patriarch had left the city and no one had yet been appointed to take his place, the papal legate was chosen to act in his stead. Cardinal Peter of Capua had been an uneasy but apparently voiceless spectator of the Crusaders' actions ever since the attack on Zara. He may now have felt that he was justifying his presence with the fleet and the army. By crowning the new Latin Emperor of Constantinople, he at least established the Pope's authority over both the Emperor, the Cathedral and the whole eastern church.

As for the Pope himself, when the news finally reached him of the manner in which Constantinople had been taken, his indignation could not be contained. Everything that he had feared and mistrusted about the enterprise (ever since it had fallen into the hands of the Venetians) had come to pass. He saw his dream of a great Crusade against the heathen disappear like smoke in the Byzantine wind. He realised that nothing would ever re-establish the army as a composite unit, and that nothing would now prevent the barons from carving up the remnants of the Byzantine Empire for themselves. Even the fact that, at long last, the schism between eastern and western Churches was apparently healed could not assuage his anger and his despair. As he wrote in one of many letters which he despatched to Baldwin in Constantinople after its capture:

"You took upon yourselves the duty of delivering the Holy Land from the Infidel. You were forbidden under pain of excommunication from attacking any Christian lands, unless they refused you passage or would not help you (and even then, you were to do nothing contrary to the wishes of my legate). You had no claims or pretensions to the lands of Greece. You were under the most solemn vows of Our Lord—and yet you have totally disregarded these vows. It was not against the Infidel but against Christians that you drew your sword. It was not Jerusalem that you captured but Constantinople. It was not heavenly riches upon which your minds were set, but earthly ones. But far and above all of this, nothing has been sacred to you—neither age nor sex. In the eyes of the whole world you have abandoned yourselves to debauchery, adultery and prostitution. You have not only violated married women and widows, but even women and virgins whose lives were dedicated to Christ. You have looted not only the treasures of the Emperor and of citizens both rich and poor, but have despoiled the very sanctuaries of God's Church. You have broken into holy places, stolen the sacred objects of altars—even including crucifixes—and you have pillaged innumerable images and relics of the Saints. It is hardly surprising that the Greek Church, beaten down though it is, rejects any obedience to the Apostolic See. It is hardly surprising that it sees in all Latins no more than treachery and the works of the Devil, and regards all of them as curs."

Within a few months of the Latin seizure of the city, Innocent III was to learn from Catholic priests in the army of occupation that the Orthodox clergy had resolutely turned their backs upon any union of the Churches. None of the Orthodox had ever at any time contemplated such a union, but the manner in which Constantinople had been raped had reinforced their hatred of Rome.

One thing that the Crusaders and Venetians had achieved in their capture of the city was to ensure that the rift between the two major branches of Christendom would last for centuries.

They had split Christendom more conclusively than if they had been pagans, and the loathing which the Orthodox Church was to feel towards Rome was to bear its fruit in 1453. At the very moment when the Moslem Turks were bent on capturing the city, Lucas Notaras, one of the last great statesmen whom Constantinople was to produce, could still remark: "Better the Sultan's turban than the Cardinal's hat." Such was the hatred that the Fourth Crusade inspired, and such was the outlook it produced, that a Greek Christian two and a half centuries later would rather have embraced Mohammedanism than Union with the Church of Rome.

As for the Venetians, the Pope's indignation knew no bounds. It was they, he pointed out, who had deliberately deflected a Crusading army designed to make war upon the Saracens. "You despised my legate," he continued, "and treated my excommunication of you with contempt. You have broken your Christian vows, and have despoiled the Churches and their treasures ... Tell me, if you can, how you can ever redeem yourselves—you who have turned aside a Christian army destined for the Holy Land? With this great and powerful army not only Jerusalem but even part of Babylon might have been captured. The proof of this is that an army which could so easily take Greece and Constantinople could equally well have captured Alexandria and the Holy Land from the infidels." His words fell on indifferent ears. Rome was a long way away, and in any case neither Dandolo nor his fellow-Venetians regarded the Pope as any more than another temporal ruler.*

The Pope's own legate, Cardinal Peter of Capua, was no less castigated for his part in the expedition. Innocent III even went so far as to say that he believed the Cardinal had been privy to the plot all along. This is impossible to believe, and indeed the Doge and Boniface and the other leaders had had so little to do with the Papal legate since he had first joined the expedition that it is inconceivable he was one of the conspirators. But in the Pope's eyes the Cardinal's worst sin was that he had absolved the Crusaders from their vow to proceed to the Holy Land, and had even lifted the sentence of excommunication from the Venetians. Presumably he had felt that the Pope would be sufficiently pleased at the subjection of the Orthodox Church to Rome as to forgive the way in which it had been done.

But it was the very manner in which it had been done that filled Innocent with rage. When he had first received the news from Baldwin that the eastern Church now accepted Union, and that the age-old schism was healed, he had written expressing his approval and enthusiasm. But when he learned the true details of the capture of Constantinople, and of the sack that had followed it, he recoiled in horror. Innocent III was too distinguished a human being to believe that 'the end justifies the means'. The fact remained that he was powerless to do any more than express his violent disapproval of every action that had been taken since the fleet had left Venice. His powerlessness was very clearly reflected in the fact that he now learned the Venetians had calmly appointed a fellow-Venetian, Thomas Morosini, to be the new Patriarch of Constantinople. They had done this without even bothering to consult the Pope, merely allowing him to be informed when their action was a *fait accompli*.

Meanwhile the dismemberment and reapportioning of the Byzantine Empire engaged the attention of the victors. The Venetians took the three-eighths of Constantinople which had been part of their price—and made sure that their share included Santa Sophia and the rich area around the Cathedral. Dandolo, under his sumptuous title of 'Duke of Dalmatia and Croatia, and Lord of one quarter and a half of the Roman Empire' was given the further Byzantine title of 'Despot' and wore the imperial buskins just as if he was co-emperor. He quickly made sure that those parts of the Empire which would be useful to Venice were apportioned to her—the western, or Ionian, coastline of Greece, together with the Ionian Islands, the ports on the northern side of the Sea of Marmora, the Greek Peloponnese or such ports on its coast as Venice might want, the islands of Andros, Euboea and Naxos, Gallipoli, and the great inland trading city of Adrianople.

As against these tangible and practical assets, the inheritance of the Emperor Baldwin was considerably less promising. It was true that all of Thrace was his, but much of it would need to be conquered, or at least compelled by a show of strength to recognise him as emperor. A further hazard to his overlordship of Thrace was the fact that two ex-emperors were still in his domains—Murtzuphlus, and Alexius III, the man whose occupancy of the throne had been the excuse for the army's first attack on the city. Both these ex-emperors had their followers and both would be unlikely to submit without a fight, knowing the fate that would inevitably be in store for them. Apart from Thrace, the Emperor Baldwin was to rule over the provinces of Bithynia and Mysia as far south as Mount Olympus, and a number of the eastern Aegean Islands, among them Lesbos, Chios, Samos and Cos. Since they were all on the fringe of Turkish-occupied Asia Minor, they, too, were likely to be more of a liability than an asset.

As for Boniface, his territory was to include the central and eastern parts of continental Greece (largely unproductive), the island of Crete, and 'the Roman territory of Asia Minor'. Since nearly all Asia Minor, with the exception of a few Byzantine enclaves like Nicea and Trebizond, was now in the hands of the Turks, this gift was a hollow one. Boniface certainly did not command enough troops to dream of undertaking a full-scale campaign against the Turks.

Having paid homage to Baldwin as his lord, Boniface quickly began agitating for a better share of land. He pointed out that since he was married to the sister of the King of Hungary it would be convenient for him to rule the principality of Thessalonica, as it adjoined the lands of his brother-in-law. In return, he was prepared to concede his rights to the somewhat problematical territory in Asia Minor.

Baldwin had no wish to have this dangerous rival on the mainland just south of his own territory and argued forcibly against any change in the agreement. Boniface, however, circumvented him and secured the backing of the Venetians for his claim, with the result that Baldwin was forced to give way and Boniface became ruler of Thessalonica and its important industrial and trading city of Salonica. It is worth remarking that, in exchange for the support of Doge Dandolo and the Venetians, Boniface sold them the island of Crete. It was a useful acquisition on their part, and one which they were to turn to their advantage in the centuries to come.

Already the ruin of a structure that had survived—although with shifting fortunes—ever since the reign of Constantine was complete. Greece and the Aegean Islands, the territories of eastern Europe, and the remnants of the Empire in Asia Minor had lost their central control. Divided into petty feudal kingdoms, they were destined to collapse into an anarchy that would not be resolved until the Ottoman Empire imposed its iron hand upon them.

The Latin 'Empire of Romania', as it was called, was unworkable from the very start. Its constitution was impracticable; it was hampered by its dependence on Venice; by its lack of a fleet, and by its ruined financial position. To add to the problems, it was not long before the rift between Baldwin and Boniface openly declared itself. Upon Baldwin's preparing to march into Thrace to establish his hold over his territory, and to destroy Murtzuphlus and Alexius III, Boniface declined to accompany him—declaring that for his part he wanted to go to Salonica to secure his new principality. Dandolo, meanwhile, was left behind in Constantinople as virtual ruler of the city.

Baldwin, having failed to secure Boniface's assistance, himself marched south to Salonica. His rival promptly made his way north and began besieging the city of Adrianople—technically part of Venice's spoils from the conquest. Let loose upon the broad and unfamiliar lands of eastern Europe, the new emperor and his principal vassal were behaving in the same arrogant and ignorant way as did the feudal barons in Europe. War was all they understood—and only petty war at that. Any conception of long-term policies, or of campaigns designed to secure and hold down huge territories, was beyond their primitive military education. Yet these were the men who had inherited the Byzantine Empire—an empire that had survived over centuries through statecraft, guile and an understanding of the ancient Roman principles of government.

The months following the conquest of the city might well have served as an inspiration for those words of W. B. Yeats:

Things fall apart; the centre cannot hold;
Mere anarchy is loosed upon the world,
The blood-dimmed tide is loosed, and everywhere
The ceremony of innocence is drowned;
The best lack all conviction, while the worst
Are full of passionate intensity." *

The dispute between the Emperor Baldwin and Boniface of Montferrat was finally settled by Dandolo. So great was the latter's power and influence during this period that he seems to have had little difficulty in getting both of these high-handed men to come to his council table, and to accept his decision. The fact was that, despite everything that had happened, the Venetians still controlled Constantinople. They were the masters of its ruler and of all the army, by virtue of the fact that they alone had the shipping without which the city could not exist. Only the Venetians understood the complexities of the eastern Empire, the Aegean and the Levant. The Belgians, French, Northern Italians and Germans who made up the bulk of the Crusading nobility, were like children in their hands. Villehardouin (who was often involved in the transactions taking place during this period) reveals quite clearly that, although Baldwin was technically the emperor, Boniface was the more powerful and impressive figure. Without intending it, he shows also that the real power lay in the hands of Dandolo.

When the first struggle for power between Baldwin and Boniface was resolved (with the definite agreement that Boniface was now ruler of the principality of Salonica), it might have seemed that the main problems of the reorganisation of the Empire were resolved. This was far from the case, even though the one Greek emperor who had shown fire and spirit was soon in the hands of the Latins.

Murtzuphlus, betrayed and forsaken by his followers, was tricked and captured by the sinister Alexius III. The latter, who seems to have been one of the most despicable characters in history, lured Murtzuphlus to a conference with the suggestion that the two of them, ex-emperors both, should combine their fortunes and their interests. Once Murtzuphlus had arrived he was, in the words of Villehardouin, "hurled to the ground and blinded". (Even at this late stage in his fortunes Alexius does not seem to have had the necessary courage to have his enemies killed outright.)

Captured by the forces of Baldwin, who were advancing into northern Thrace to secure the land and the cities for the new emperor, Murtzuphlus was brought back in chains to Constantinople. As the murderer of the Fourth Crusade's protégé, the young Alexius, Murtzuphlus had no hope of clemency. He was ceremonially conducted to the Forum of the Bull before the citizens of Constantinople and the soldiers of the Fourth Crusade. "And once there," says Nicetas, "he was led to the top of the high tower which stands in the centre of this Forum—and was cast to the ground." Thus perished Murtzuphlus, last Greek Emperor of Constantinople before the Latin conquest.

The fate of his adversary the ex-Emperor Alexius III was far better than he deserved. It is impossible to have any sympathy with this weak-willed debauchee who had reduced the city to ruin, and who had never displayed any courage in its defence. Fleeing from Thrace, after a brief period as a prisoner of Boniface of Montferrat, he reached Asia Minor where he very soon began conspiring against his own son-in-law, Theodore Lascaris, for the Kingdom of Nicea. Captured and imprisoned, he ended his days in a Nicean monastery—a far kinder fate than those that he had prepared for either his predecessor or his successor on the throne of Constantinople.

As the year 1204 drew to a close, one of the greatest revolutions in European history had taken place—sordid, sinister and without parallel. The whole of the ancient eastern empire, the bastion of Christendom for 900 years, had been dismantled and lay in ruins. In its place, like maggots on a corpse, swarmed the petty and provincial baronies and principalities that owed their origin to the backward states of western Europe.

Constantinople and the Byzantine Empire had straddled the seas dividing Europe from Asia for centuries, and had withstood the shocks of many warring cultures and nations. Now, not unlike the Colossus of Rhodes, this giant monument to the Greek genius lay broken in pieces. It is recorded that when the famous Colossus of Rhodes was overthrown by an earthquake "it was sold to a scrap-metal dealer who had to use 900 camels to carry it away".* The same thing was now happening to that far greater Colossus, the Byzantine Empire. The remnants of its gigantic limbs have never to this day been reassembled, let alone cast into a satisfactory new mould.

18

LANDSCAPE WITH RUINS

THE conquest brought little happiness to the main protagonists in the drama. Within three years of the capture of Constantinople, the new emperor, Baldwin, the Doge, Enrico Dandolo, and Boniface, Marquis of Montferrat, were all dead—Baldwin within less than a year of his accession to the throne. In the spring of 1205, with nearly all the Greeks in Thrace in revolt against him, Baldwin led out his troops to try and subdue his inheritance. Villehardouin tells us that "the Greeks, who were always perfidious by nature, harboured thoughts of treachery in their hearts". He does not seem to wonder why the Greeks should ever have been expected to submit willingly to the rule of these Latin Crusaders.

"Seeing that the French were widely scattered throughout the land and were all occupied with their own affairs, the Greeks thought they could overcome them by craft and double-dealing. So they sent messengers secretly to King Johanitza of Bulgaria (who had long been their enemy and indeed was technically still at war with them) saying they would make him emperor if he would come to their aid . . ."

One of the reasons that prompted what has been called this "Unnatural alliance between Greeks and Bulgarians"* was the claim of the Latin Patriarch, Thomas Morosini, to jurisdiction over the Bulgarian Orthodox Church. Now the latter, like the Orthodox Church of Russia, was a direct offshoot of the Byzantine Church and was adamant at refusing to accept the claims of the Papacy. Greeks and Bulgars were thus wedded together for the first time against an outside enemy, an enemy not only of their lands but of their Faith. At the Battle of Adrianople, on April 15th, 1205, the army under Baldwin was almost annihilated by a combined Greek and Bulgarian force, and the Emperor himself was captured. Taken to the Bulgarian capital of Tirnovo, Baldwin was imprisoned in a tower and later executed. According to one contemporary account, his hands and feet were cut off and he was thrown into a valley, where it took him three days to die. So perished Count Baldwin of Flanders and Hainault, Baldwin I of the Latin Empire of Romania. He was succeeded by his brother Henri, a capable and energetic man who did his best to maintain a hopeless inheritance.

A few months later, in June 1205, Doge Dandolo died peacefully in the palace of Boucoleon. The man who more than any other had been responsible for the diversion of the Fourth Crusade to Constantinople, who had duped, controlled and master-minded the leaders of the army for the purposes of Venice, did not live long enough to see the Empire of Romania disintegrate. Perhaps he had always anticipated that this would happen, but he had been rightly confident that the gains he had made for Venice would long outlast his own time. Born about 1120, this octogenarian could look back on a long life dedicated to the interests of the Republic. He had achieved more since his seventieth year than most men in a lifetime. When he had been elected Doge on January 1st, 1193, the Dalmatian coastline had been lost to Venice and had become a protectorate of the King of Hungary. In a brilliantly successful campaign Dandolo had restored Venetian authority over Dalmatia, defeating the Pisan fleet in the course of the struggle. His only failure had been his inability to subdue the ancient seaport of Zara—but he had more than made up for this by his diversion of the Crusaders to Zara in November 1202. From then on his ascendancy over the Crusade was complete, and in the capture of Constantinople he fulfilled the ambition of a lifetime. Whether there is any truth in the story that he had a personal desire for vengeance and that he had been deliberately blinded during his previous embassy to the city or whether this is legend, the fact remains that he had more than avenged Venice's previous defeat at the hands of the Byzantines. He had succeeded in destroying Venice's greatest rival for the trade of the East, and he had established a lifeline for his city consisting of most of the important islands, ports and trading bases on the route to Asia and the Levant.

As a Venetian he could die happy, conscious of having immensely furthered and strengthened the power and prosperity of the Republic. In the subsequent chronicles of Venice he was deservedly acclaimed as one of the greatest Doges of all time, a unique consolidator and promoter of his city's fortunes. To the historian concerned with the subsequent history of Europe, Dandolo's success in diverting the Fourth Crusade must be reckoned one of the greatest disasters ever to befall the continent. "Constantinople had been for centuries the strongest bulwark of defence against Asia. The men of the West had every interest to maintain and to strengthen it. Instead of doing so they virtually let loose Asia upon Europe."* The man who was mainly responsible for this disaster was buried with the Latin rites in the desecrated Cathedral of Santa Sophia. The fact that the Church of Divine Wisdom would one day be turned into a mosque was as much the doing of Doge Dandolo as it was of its ultimate conqueror, the Sultan Mehmet II.

The third principal figure in the history of the Fourth Crusade, Boniface Marquis of Montferrat, was temporarily more successful than the unfortunate Baldwin. Apart from securing his kingdom in Thessalonica, he managed to subdue a large part of continental Greece, and introduced his vassals as rulers of small separate kingdoms. The Burgundian family of La Roche were established as Dukes of Athens and of Thebes, while in the Morea the nephew of Villehardouin the historian established the Principality of Achaea. Boniface himself remained a doubtful subject of the new Emperor Henri until he succeeded in cementing an alliance with him by marrying his daughter Agnes to Henri in the spring of 1206.*

Meanwhile King Johanitza of Bulgaria continued to ravage large areas of northern Thrace, so "the Emperor Henri and the Marquis of Montferrat agreed to meet at the end of summer, in the month of October 1207, and make war together on the King. They parted good friends and in good spirits, the Marquis making his way back to Mosynopolis and the Emperor returning to Constantinople . . ." A few days later Boniface was caught by the Bulgarians in a defile near the city, and was mortally wounded. "The few men who were with him at the time were all killed, and the Bulgarians cut off the Marquis's head and sent it to King Johanitza . . ."

Villehardouin ends his history of the Fourth Crusade with the death of Boniface, adding: "Alas, what a terrible disaster this was for the Emperor Henri and for everyone in the Empire, whether French or Venetian, to lose so great a man in such a tragic way. He was one of the finest and noblest of all the barons, and one of the bravest men in the world!"

His death merely served to confirm the fact that there was little or no chance of the Latin Empire of Romania ever taking root in the ruins of Byzantium. (Death in battle or disease had already killed off many of the other major participants in the Fourth Crusade.) Despite the fact that the Emperor Henri was a far abler man than his brother—indeed, the only able Latin Emperor in the brief history of that absurd feudal improvisation —there was no chance of such an unnatural graft taking root upon the stem of a civilisation so alien to feudal Europe.

Although the Emperor Henri managed to save the Latin Empire for ten years by an exercise of tolerance towards the Orthodox Church unusual in a Latin, and by an energetic efficiency that had been lacking in his brother, there was no possibility of preserving it intact. The Venetians in their wisdom had taken as their share only the places that they knew they could successfully use and—by their sea-power—retain. Carved up into pathetic fiefs among quarrelling barons and knights, the fabric of the ancient Empire quickly disintegrated.

The Greeks, meanwhile, refusing to acknowledge either the faith or the rule of the conquerors, set up three separate kingdoms—all of which claimed for themselves the inheritance of the Byzantine Empire. In Epirus, a district extending from Naupactus (better known today as Lepanto) in the Gulf of Patras to Durazzo in Albania, a bastard of the Angeli dynasty of Byzantine Emperors set up a Greek principality; this ultimately absorbed the Thessalonica kingdom that Boniface had carved out for himself. Far away on the shores of the Black

Sea, descendants of the earlier Comneni dynasty of Emperors established the extraordinary small kingdom of Trebizond. Despite several sieges, despite the hostility of Genoese traders eager to establish a monopoly in the Black Sea trade, and despite the occupation of nearly all Asia Minor by the Turks, the kingdom of the Comneni managed to survive until 1461. Eight years after Constantinople had fallen to the Turks, Trebizond was finally captured by the same victorious Sultan, Mehmet II.

The third Greek splinter-kingdom arising from the Latin conquest was the one that was ultimately to regain Constantinople for the Greeks. This was the 'Empire of Nicea' established by Theodore Lascaris and his family. It was here that the new Greek Patriarch was elected, and here therefore that the new centre of the Orthodox Church was established. Within two years of the conquest of Constantinople, the Crusaders were happy to conclude a peace treaty with Lascaris, leaving him in possession of all that remained of the ancient Greek territories in Asia Minor. Under his successor, the remarkable John Vatatzes, nearly the whole of western Asia Minor was regained from the Turks by the Greeks.

Meanwhile, throughout ruined Greece, on promontories and headlands, and in distant parts of the Morea, there proliferated those extraordinary small feudal kingdoms and petty baronies that derived from the wreck of the ancient Empire. The ruins of their castles can still be seen, dominating some silent cove or bay, or overhanging a 'romantic' pass through angular silver cliffs. Jousting and the ritual of the Courts of Love invaded Greek territories—exotic grafts that were doomed to perish in so different a soil and climate. Seneschals, Grand Butlers, Grand Constables, these western titles resounded strangely and for a brief while on the Byzantine air—and then were gone.

In the years immediately following the conquest, many western knights hastened to carve out small kingdoms for themselves, and fiefs in Greece and eastern Europe. Some, who had lost their inheritances in Syria to the infidel, sailed for Constantinople and Greece to re-establish their fortunes. Others, who had once thought of crusading in Outremer, turned aside to find for themselves wealth and estates in eastern Europe. The breakdown of the Empire was soon complete, and it was hardly surprising that even the surviving trunk and head —Thrace and Constantinople—were not sufficiently coordinated to be able to withstand the first real attack made upon them.

In 1261, only fifty-seven years after the conquest of the city, Constantinople fell to the forces of Michael Palaeologus, Greek ruler of the kingdom of Nicea. The last Latin emperor, Baldwin II, fled—and with him went the Latin Patriarch and the Venetian settlers. Constantinople was once more restored to a Greek dynasty and the Orthodox Church, as its Patriarch returned to Santa Sophia. It seemed for a moment as if the glories of the past might yet return. "The exile of the Greek monarchy and of its Church in Nicea had, as it were, spiritually purified the State of Nicea and had given it a national character which Constantinople no longer possessed . . . A new spirit was born there, and it was to this spirit that the restored Byzantine Empire was to owe for two more centuries, a life which was not always humble and threatened."*

The fact remained that the restored Byzantine State, even though it endured until the mid-fifteenth century, was no more than a travesty of its former self. The Crusaders and the Venetians had done their work. Even though they were expelled from the city, they still controlled most of Greece, while the Genoese and Venetians between them held nearly all the important islands of the Aegean. As for the brief half-century of the Latin Empire its epitaph was best written by Gregorovius: "A creation of western European crusading knights, of the selfish trade-policy of the Venetians, and of the hierarchical idea of the papacy, it fell after a miserable existence of fifty-seven years, leaving behind it no other trace than destruction and anarchy. That deformed chivalrous feudal state of the Latins belongs to the most worthless phenomena of history."

The subsequent history of the city and of the remnant of the Empire is one of slow decline. Even though there was a great artistic revival during the fourteenth century, Constantinople's fate was sealed. The city that had once held over a million inhabitants became sparsely populated, great sections of it being turned over into vegetable gardens, orchards and farming plots. Whole quarters had disappeared, the beautiful palace of Boucoleon lay in ruins—largely because the last Latin emperor had stripped all the lead off its roof in an effort to pay his debts. More than half the churches were deserted or destroyed.

By the fourteenth century the Arab geographer Abulfeda could remark that there were "sown fields within the city and many ruined houses." The traveller Gonzales de Clavijo who visited Constantinople in the early fifteenth century (some fifty years before the Turkish conquest), wrote that most of the great palaces, churches and monasteries were in ruin, adding, "But it is clear that once upon a time, when Constantinople was in its pristine state, it was among the noblest cities in the world." Coming two centuries after the Latin conquest he could hardly envisage the fabulous capital that had made Venetians and Crusaders alike catch their breath in awe.

By the mid-fourteenth century little or nothing was left of the city's ancient splendour. When the Emperor John VI Cantacuzenus and his consort were crowned, a foreign visitor remarked that not even the jewels in the imperial diadems were real. Imitation pearls and pastes had replaced the pearls, innumerable diamonds, emeralds and rubies of the past. Pewter and earthenware served instead of the silver of ancient days, and at the coronation banquet brass did duty for what had once been the imperial gold plate. Yet there was a dignity about the last of these Byzantine emperors, as the great Greek poet of Alexandria, C. P. Cavafy, wrote:

> *Nothing*
> *That is mean or that is unseemly*
> *Do they have in my eyes, those little bits*
> *Of coloured glass. They seem on the contrary*
> *Like a sorrowful protestation*
> *Against the unjust misfortune of those being crowned.**

But however unjust the misfortune of these later emperors and their subjects, nothing could save the city. The Bulgarians under a succession of able sovereigns had become a formidable power in the Balkan peninsula, while, by the middle of the fourteenth century, the rise of the Serbian Empire menaced even Constantinople itself. Western Europe also remained hostile to the ancient kingdom, for the idea of re-establishing the Latin Empire of Romania was never entirely abandoned.

But the main danger came from the Turks, who under their great leader Osman were soon once more in control of nearly all Asia Minor, having captured the great city of Brusa in 1326 and Nicea in 1329. Osman, founder of the Ottoman dynasty, welded the scattered forces of innumerable small Turkish tribal leaders into a sword that was ultimately to cut deep into the Christian world.

"God the All-Powerful," runs an Arabic saying, "has an army which he has named the Turks. Whenever he is angry with a people, he lets loose his army upon them." The main consequence of the conquest of Constantinople by the Crusaders in 1204 was to ensure that sooner or later the Turks would over-run eastern Europe. With the Byzantine Empire broken and dismantled, there was nothing to stand in their way. Before the end of the fourteenth century this had happened. The Turkish army was swarming over Europe; the Serbians and Bulgarians had been crushed; Albania invaded; and Adrianople made the Turkish capital. By the mid-fifteenth century the Duchy of Athens had fallen to the Turks as had the principality of the Morea. Nothing remained but the city itself.

It has been truly said that "Constantinople constituted the Empire, occasionally it reconstituted the Empire, sometimes it was the whole Empire". But at last, in the face of an immense army and the genius of Mehmet II, the last days of Constantinople had come. The city fell for the second time in its history on May 29th, 1453, its last Emperor Constantine IX dying heroically in the forefront of the battle, as the Turkish soldiers swarmed over the walls. For the second time, Constantinople was abandoned for three days to fire and the sword. But, despite the inevitable rapine and pillage, the behaviour of the Moslem conqueror contrasted more than favourably with that of the Christian army of the Fourth Crusade.

At long last, after twelve hundred years of astounding history and of outstanding cultural achievement, the Byzantine Empire was finally and forever extinguished. Its epitaph was spoken by the Sultan himself, as he rode through the twice-devastated city and contemplated the ruins of the ancient imperial palace. The melancholy of the gigantic broken columns and of the decaying buildings in the city that he had captured, reminded him of the lines which the Persian poet Sa'dí had written on the mutability of human fortune:

> *Now the spider weaves the curtains in the palace*
> *Of the Caesars,*
> *Now the owl calls the night watches in the*
> *towers of Afrasiab.*

APPENDIX

THE principal sources for any history of the Fourth Crusade must inevitably be the records left by three eyewitnesses of the events. These are: the Comte de Villehardouin; Robert de Clari; and the Byzantine nobleman, Nicetas. There are a number of other subsidiary sources, among them the monk Gunther (*Historia Constantinopolitana*), the letters of Pope Innocent III, the history written by George Acropolites, and the work of Ernoul or 'Bernard the Treasurer', which is one of the old French continuations of the history of Outremer by William of Tyre.

In the past, historians have tended to take the work of Villehardouin (*La Conquête de Constantinople*, ed. Faral, 2 vols., Paris, 1938–9) as the most trustworthy. This may perhaps be ascribed to the fact that Villehardouin gives us the fullest account of the Crusade, and that his history is 'from the inside' —since he was one of the protagonists in the enterprise. It is surprising, however, to find that even as late as 1963, Mr. R. B. Shaw in his translation of Villehardouin's chronicle (Penguin Classics: *Chronicles of the Crusades*) can write: "... He gives on the whole a very fair and honest account of an enterprise that began so well and ended so disastrously."

Villehardouin, in fact, was a highly biased reporter. Like the other participants in the Crusade, he had come under the Pope's displeasure—and excommunication—for his part in the attack on Zara. Subsequently, he was one of the principal go-betweens used by the Doge, Enrico Dandolo, and Boniface, Marquis of Montferrat, during the negotiations with the Byzantines.

It cannot be denied that Villehardouin's account is highly readable and, for its period, of considerable historical distinction. He sees things both as a soldier and a statesman, and his records of the conferences of the great bear all the hallmark of sincerity. At the same time, one must often be compelled to treat his words with circumspection. It is not so much that he is a guileful writer, but that he is an honest and ingenuous soldier, who tends to believe implicitly the facts of a matter as they are told him by others. Thus, one can see that in some of the negotiations to which he was party, the Comte de Ville-hardouin was being used as a tool by men considerably less scrupulous than he. When the Doge, or Boniface, employed him as an emissary, Villehardouin seems to have totally accepted the account of affairs as they were given to him by his superiors. His dislike of the Greeks and their 'trickery' inevit-ably brings to mind the war memoirs of distinguished soldiers in later centuries, who have had to deal with a conquered foe—and who have found it difficult to understand that the con-quered will use whatever means they can to survive and, if possible, to rise again.

Biased though it is, Villehardouin's account of the siege of Constantinople, and of the events leading up to it, is particularly invaluable regarding military affairs and the conduct of the campaign. Where it must be treated with reservation is in matters of policy, or in anything connected with the real reasons for the diversion of the Crusade.

Villehardouin, of course, had no knowledge of the Venetians' treaty with the Sultan of Egypt, and his ignorance of this matter inevitably makes him blind to the real purposes of Doge Dandolo. One can almost equally be sure that he had no knowledge of the plot between Philip of Swabia and Boniface, Marquis of Montferrat, (which had been hatched long before Villehardouin himself ever reached Venice). Valuable as his account is, it must always be treated with two major reserva-tions: that the author was unaware of the designs of the Doge and the other participants in the plot; and that, having once broken his Crusading oaths in the attack on Zara, he was con-cerned to excuse himself and the other Crusaders wherever possible.

The second French account, that of Robert de Clari (*La Con-quête de Constantinople*, ed. Lauer, Paris, 1924), is completely unlike Villehardouin's in that it is the work of a simple man with no axe to grind. In many respects it must be treated with reservation, for de Clari reports many things which he could not have known about, and records discussions and conversations which took place when he was not present. His, in fact, is a typical soldier's story, being a mixture of camp gossip, rumour and conjecture. But when he comes to describe events which he witnessed himself, actions in which he took part, or the effect produced upon him by his first views of Constantinople, then he is a vivid and fascinating source of information.

Similarly, his account of how the ordinary soldiers felt at the various meetings that took place in Venice, Zara, Corfu and Constantinople are honest and reliable. The way he describes the reactions of the troops, as they are step-by-step committed to the attack, has all the ring of authenticity. De Clari does not know what has taken place at the conferences of the great, but he does show us how the army responded to the orders and instructions of its senior officers. In this respect, therefore, his history counterbalances that of Villehardouin. While the one gives us the official story, as it were, of the whole disastrous expedition, de Clari presents us with the soldier's eye-view of events.

The main Greek authority for the history of the Latin conquest is Nicetas Choniates. Gibbon has this footnote about him: "Nicetas was of Chonae in Phrygia (the old Colossae of St. Paul); he raised himself to the honours of senator, judge of the veil, and great logothete; beheld the fall of the empire, retired to Nicea, and composed an elaborate history from the death of Alexius Comnenus to the reign of Henry." One may add to this that he was secretary to the Emperor Isaac Angelus, and accompanied him on an expedition in the field against the Wallachs and Bulgars in 1187. When the blinded Isaac and his son Alexius were restored to the throne Nicetas became Great Logothete, a position from which he was dismissed by the usurper Murtzuphlus.

Nicetas is a conservative of the old school, a patriot and a man of deep religious spirit. His work is, in a sense, a cry of pain and shame—pain at the destruction of the city and the

Empire, and shame at the way in which the later emperors and their courtiers conducted themselves. Sir Edwin Pears described him as "imbued with a religious spirit—religious in the sense that he believes that God rules the world and will punish national immorality".

Although Nicetas was in Isaac's court and one of his ministers, he has little good to say either of him or of his son. But when he comes to writing about Murtzuphlus one must suspect him of personal bias. He can find no redeeming quality in this last Byzantine emperor—even though Murtzuphlus was the only emperor during this period to show something of the ancient 'Roman' spirit.

But Nicetas's account of the events leading up to the conquest, and of the conquest itself, is invaluable. Here we have the record of a man who was at the very heart of events on the Greek side. Although one must allow for his conservative and religious bias, yet his account is a fair one. Much though he may loathe the Latins who sacked and conquered his city, he is at pains to point out that it was the corruption of the Byzantines themselves that led to their downfall. Historian, art-lover and aristocrat, Nicetas could find no words too bad to describe the Latins or their behaviour. It is from Nicetas that we learn the details of some of the works of art which were destroyed during the sack of the city.

Gibbon wrote of him that "the boasted taste of Nicetas was no more than affectation and vanity". How Gibbon, even with his notorious dislike of almost everything Byzantine, could write this after reading Nicetas's description of the statue of Helen of Troy must remain a puzzle. Certainly, there is a querulous note running through Nicetas's history, and this may perhaps account for Gibbon's dislike of the Greek author. But in view of the fact that Nicetas has lost not only his city but his home, and his whole way of life in the Latin conquest, one must feel some sympathy for the old historian. Despite its defects, his work presents us with the clearest picture of Constantinople and the Empire in the last days before its fall.

NOTES

Chapter One

Page 23. Sir Ernest Barker, 'The Crusades', in the Encyclopaedia Britannica, 14th Edition. A concise and masterly summary of the Fourth Crusade.

Page 26. Wilhelm Ensslin, *The Emperor and Imperial administration: Byzantium*, 1949, edited by N. H. Bayes and H. St. L. B. Moss. I am greatly indebted to this "Introduction to East Roman Civilization" for much of the background material used in the description of Constantinople.

Chapter Two

Page 37. 'Byzantine Art', in *Byzantium*, 1949. An illuminating summary by Charles Diehl of Byzantine culture and artistic achievements.

Page 38. Quotation from 'Sailing to Byzantium' by W. B. Yeats, *Collected Poems*, 1965, quoted by permission of Mr. M. B. Yeats and Macmillan and Co. Ltd.

Page 38. Nicetas. *Historia.* Ed. 1835.

Page 39. Robert Liddell, *Byzantium and Istanbul*, 1956.

Page 42. Sir Edwin Pears, *The Fall of Constantinople.* 1886.

Chapter Three

Page 44. T. Smith, Introduction to *The Chronicle of Geoffrey de Villehardouin*, 1829.

Page 46. Quotation from 'Easter 1916' by W. B. Yeats, *Collected Poems*, 1965, published by Macmillan.

Page 47. Villehardouin.

Chapter Four

Page 51. For a full assessment of the ramifications behind the Fourth Crusade, its organisation and objective, see: Sir Steven Runciman, *History of the Crusades*, Vol. 3, pp. 107 *et seq*. Also Sir Edwin Pears, *The Fall of Constantinople*, pp. 227 *et seq*.

Page 53. Robert de Clari gives the number of the Crusaders as "4,000 knights and 100,000 foot soldiers", while Nicetas Choniates gives the figures as "1,000 knights and 30,000 Crusaders". Villehardouin's figures are the more trustworthy.

Page 55. V. Pears, p. ix *et seq.*, and Runciman, p. 113. Of the original sources which indicate a definite agreement between the Venetians and the Egyptians, the most interesting—if not conclusive —account is that of 'Ernoul' or Bernard the Treasurer (many versions from the late twelfth century onwards). Hopf in *Geschichte Griechenlands* states positively that there was such a treaty, but gives no sources. The *Historia Constantinopolitana* by the Cistercian monk, Gunther, indicates collusion between Cairo and Venice. Gunther was a contemporary, dying in 1210. It is important to bear in mind that there is no *evidence* of this treaty, although there is evidence of a treaty between the Venetians and the Egyptians in 1208.

Page 55. See the two MSS. quoted by Buchon in *Le Livre de la Conqueste*, Paris, 1845.

Illustration between pp. 56–57.

The Attack on Zara. Tintoretto working in the 16th century depicts cannons, and soldiers armed with arquebuses. both of course unknown in 1202.

Page 58. 36,000 marks according to de Clari.

Page 61. In itself, the concession that Dandolo hereby enforced from the Republic was unique. There was normally no question of the Doge's office being subject to the hereditary principle.

Chapter Five

Page 71. For much of the information concerning the arms and armour of this period I am indebted to C. J. Ffoulkes's *The Armourer and his Craft*, London, 1912. Also to Sir G. F. Laking's *A Record of European Armour and Arms*, London, 1920.

Page 75. In 1453, when the Sultan Mehmet II finally captured the city at the head of the Turkish forces, the tower and its defences were so strong that he despaired of attacking it. Instead, he had his ships dragged overland from Tophane and launched in the area of the Modern Kasimpaşa. Mehmet, however, did not have anything approaching the sea-power of the Venetians and, at the time of his attack on Constantinople, the suburb of Galata had itself been turned into a separate walled city.

Page 75. Nicetas has a permanent bias against the Comneni emperors, but there is no real reason to believe that in his estimation of the individual actors in this drama he was not as accurate as French writers like de Clari and Villehardouin. The latter, in any case, had no way of knowing what was going on in the minds of the Greeks.

Chapter Six

Page 91. *The Byzantines* by D. Talbot Rice, London, 1962.

Chapter Seven

Page 95. Quotation from 'The Curassiers of the Frontier' by Robert Graves, *Collected Poems*, 1965, published by Cassell and Co. Ltd. Quoted by permission of International Authors, N. V.

Page 95. Orderic Vitalis. This account is substantiated by other historians of the city such as Anna Comnena, Cedrenus and Gotselinus.

Page 97. Pears, *The Fall of Constantinople*, 1886.

Chapter Eight

Page 103. An eleventh-century poem celebrating Digenes Akrites, ed. John Mavrogordato, Oxford, 1956.

Page 103. It seems clear from the styles of Villehardouin's memoirs that they were dictated. There is no conclusive manuscript evidence that he could write.

Chapter Nine

Page 114. Alexius III had, in fact, made his way to Mosynopolis. This has been identified with a small village just west of Adrianople.

Page 118. Nicetas, who can never find anything creditable to say about Alexius IV, maintains that the fire occurred *before* he had left Constantinople with the Crusaders. He pictures Alexius gloating over the flames like Nero. Villehardouin, however, who was in a better position to know the whereabouts of the Emperor (and had no personal bias against him), maintains that it occurred while Alexius was away in Thrace. His view is confirmed by other authorities.

Chapter Ten

Page 125. Gunther, *Historia Constantinopolitana*, X.

Page 129. The Byzantines by D. Talbot Rice, 1962.

Chapter Eleven

Page 131. Alexius Ducas, nicknamed Murtzuphlus, had been crowned as Alexius V. I have continued to refer to him as 'Murtzuphlus' in order to avoid confusion between him, Alexius IV (now dead), and Alexius III, the ex-Emperor, now a refugee in Thracian Mosynopolis.

Page 133. The Chronicle of Novgorod, 96. Neither Nicetas, Villehardouin, nor de Clari give any indication that Alexius had betrayed the Byzantines. Nevertheless, knowing Alexius's position at that moment and his total dependence upon his Venetian and Crusader friends, it seems quite possible that he may have warned them of the impending attack.

Page 135. It has been calculated from the evidence of the reser-

voirs that remain, and from the sites of the ancient cisterns, that
they must have held about 1,000,000, cubic metres.

Page 136. The inscription is quoted by Robert Liddell in *Byzantium and Istanbul,* 1956.

Page 137. Benjamin of Tudela, *Itinerary,* trans. M. N. Adler, 1907.

Page 139. From Runciman, *The Fall of Constantinople 1453,* 1965.

Page 140. Quoted from Alexander van Millingen, *Constantinople,*
1929.

Chapters Twelve and Thirteen

For the information contained in these chapters I have combined
Villehardouin's and de Clari's accounts, trusting the one where it is
a matter of policy and strategy, and the other where he was an
eyewitness of events.

Page 152. The desertion of Murtzuphlus's cavalry in the face of
inferior forces suggests not only a breakdown in morale—it is possible
that there was a deliberate conspiracy to abandon the Emperor at
the first opportunity.

Chapter Fourteen

Page 160. Persia and the Greeks, The Defence of the West 546-478 B.C.,
by A. R. Burn, 1962.

Page 163. This quotation from Thomas Carlyle's *The French
Revolution* provides an interesting parallel to the contemporary
account of Nicetas.

Page 166. Art of the Byzantine Era by D. Talbot Rice, 1963.

Chapter Fifteen

Nicetas is our authority for the description of some of the individual works of art that were destroyed. Both Villehardouin and de
Clari, while full of wonder at the wealth of the city, omit to mention
the wholesale destruction of works of art.

Chapter Sixteen

Page 176. Sismondi, *Histoire de la chute de l'empire Romain,* 1835.

Page 176. Pears, *The Fall of Constantinople,* 1886.

Page 177. Now in the Victorian and Albert Museum, London,
See *The Veroli Casket* by John Beckwith, H.M.S.O., 1962.

Page 181. The account of the proceedings is taken from the *Chroni-
que de Romanie* (Buchon's *Collection de Chroniques,* 1875). It cannot be
regarded as entirely trustworthy, but would seem to reflect fairly
accurately the spirit, at least, of events during the meeting of the
electors. Neither Villehardouin nor de Clari was in a position to
know what happened. Villehardouin, however, states specifically

that no one was admitted to the Church while the election was taking place. This seems very likely. But since the Doge was at this time inhabiting Boucoleon Palace, it is quite possible that finding the electors divided on the issue *before* they entered the Church, he threw the weight of his authority behind Baldwin in advance of their deliberations. One thing is clear, there seems no doubt from any account that the Doge favoured Baldwin, and that it was his influence which secured his election against the undoubtedly stronger claims of Boniface.

Chapter Seventeen

Page 185. Letters of Pope Innocent, VIII and IX, Migne, *Patrologiae Cursus Completus, Series Latina*, Vols. CCIV–CCV.

Page 189. Quotation from 'The Second Coming', by W. B. Yeats, *Collected Poems*, 1965. Quoted by permission of Mr. M. B. Yeats and Macmillan and Co. Ltd.

Page 191. Baron de Balabre, *Rhodes of the Knights*, 1909.

Chapter Eighteen

Page 192. Runciman, *History of the Crusades*, Vol. III, 1954.

Page 194. Pears, Introduction to *The Fall of Constantinople*, 1886.

Page 194. A daughter not, of course, by his wife the Dowager Empress Margaret, but by an earlier marriage.

Page 197. C. Diehl in *Byzantium: An Introduction to East Roman Civilization*, 1948.

Page 198. Quoted, by permission, from 'Coloured Glass', in *The Poems of C. P. Cavafy*, translated by John Mavrogordato, published by the Hogarth Press Ltd., 1951.

SHORT BIBLIOGRAPHY

Acropolites, George, *Opera* (Heisenberg), 1903.
Baynes, N. H., *Byzantine Studies and other Essays*, 1955.
Baynes, N. H., and Moss H. St. L. B., *Byzantium*, 1953.
Bréhier, L., *Vie et Mort de Byzance*, 1948.
Clari, Robert de, *La Conquête de Constantinople* (ed. Lauer), 1924.
Cotelerius, *Ecclesiae Graecae Monumenta*, Vol. III.
Diehl, C. H., *Histoire de l'Empire Byzantin*, 1919.
Gibbon, Edward, *The Decline and Fall of the Roman Empire*, Ed. 1896.
Gregoire, H., 'The Diversion of the Fourth Crusade', in *Byzantion*, 1941.
Gunther, *Historia Constantinopolitana* (*Exuviae*, Riant P.).
Hamilton, J. A., *Byzantine Architecture*, 1956.
Hodgson, F. C., *The Early History of Venice*, 1901.
Hussey, J. M., *The Byzantine World*, 1957.
Innocent III, Pope, *Letters:* VIII and IX in Migne, Vols. CCIV–CCV.
Kretschmayr, H., *Geshicte Von Venedig*, 1905.
Liddell, R., *Byzantium and Istanbul*, 1956.
Longnon, J., *L'Empire Latin de Constantinople*, 1949.
Luchaire, A., *Innocent III, La Question d'Orient*, 1911.
Muñoz, A., *L'Art Byzantin*, 1906.
Nicetas (Choniates), *Historia*, ed, 1835.
Oman, C. W. C., *The History of the Art of War:* Middle Ages, 1898.
Oman C. W. C., *The Byzantine Empire*, 1892.
Ostrogorsky, G., *History of the Byzantine State*, 1956.
Pears, Sir E., *The Fall of Constantinople, 1204*, 1886.
Raynaldus, O., *Annales Ecclesiastici*, 1747–56.
Regestum Innocentii Papae super Negotio Romani Imperii (ed. F. Kempf), 1947.
Riant, P., *Exuviae Sacrae Constantinopolitanae*, 1877–8.
Rice, D. Talbot, *The Byzantines*, 1962.
Rice, D. Talbot, *The Art of Byzantium*, 1959.
Romanin, S., *Storia documentata di Venezia*, 1853.
Runciman, Sir S., *A History of the Crusades*. Vol. III, 1954.
Runciman, Sir S., *Byzantine Civilization*, 1933.
Schlumberger, G., *Byzance et Croisades*, 1927.

Sherard, P., *Constantinople*, 1965.
Simonsfeld, H., *Andrea Dandolo*, 1876.
Vasiliev, A. A., *History of the Byzantine Empire*, 1952.
Villehardouin, Geoffrey de, *La Conquête de Constantinople* (ed. Faral), 1938–9.
Devastatic Constantinopolitana: Annals Herpipolenses, XVI.
The Great Palace of the Byzantine Emperors (Oxford), 1947.

INDEX